TEACHING IN TODAY'S

CA_____TARY

SCHOOL

Merrill Titles by George L. Redman

A Casebook for Exploring Diversity in K–12 Classrooms

Teaching in Today's Classrooms: Cases from Elementary School

Teaching in Today's Classrooms: Cases from Middle and Secondary School

TEACHING IN TODAY'S CLASSROOMS

CASES FROM ELEMENTARY SCHOOL

George L. Redman
Hamline University

Merrill,
an imprint of Prentice Hall
Upper Saddle River, New Jersey   Columbus, Ohio

Library of Congress Cataloging-in-Publication Data
Redman, George
    Teaching in today's classrooms : cases from elementary school /
George L. Redman.
        p.   cm.
    Includes bibliographical references.
    ISBN 0-13-627142-1
        1. Elementary school teaching—Minnesota—Case Studies.
    2. Elementary school teachers—Training of—Minnesota.   3. Case
    method.   I.Title.
    LB1555.R43   1999
    372.1102—DC21   98-13900
                                                              CIP

Editor: Debra A. Stollenwerk
Production Editor: Mary Harlan
Design Coordinator: Karrie M. Converse
Text Design and Production Coordination: Custom Editorial Productions, Inc.
Cover Art: Kaili Sullivan, Super Stock
Cover Designer: Susan Unger
Production Manager: Pamela D. Bennett
Director of Marketing: Kevin Flanagan
Marketing Manager: Suzanne Stanton
Marketing Coordinator: Krista Groshong

This book was set in Garamond by Custom Editorial Productions, Inc., and
was printed and bound by R.R. Donnelley and Sons Company. The cover was
printed by Phoenix Color Corp.

 © 1999 by Prentice-Hall, Inc.
Simon & Schuster/A Viacom Company
Upper Saddle River, New Jersey 07458

Photo Credits: All photos supplied courtesy of Hamline University

Printed in the United States of America

10   9   8   7   6   5   4   3   2   1

ISBN: 0-13-627142-1

Prentice-Hall International (UK) Limited, *London*
Prentice-Hall of Australia Pty. Limited, *Sydney*
Prentice-Hall of Canada, Inc., *Toronto*
Prentice-Hall Hispanoamericana, S.A., *Mexico*
Prentice-Hall of India Private Limited, *New Delhi*
Prentice-Hall of Japan, Inc., *Tokyo*
Simon & Schuster Asia Pte. Ltd., *Singapore*
Editora Prentice-Hall do Brasil, Ltda., *Rio de Janeiro*

Preface

Teaching in Today's Classrooms: Cases from Elementary School is a text supplement for use in methods and foundations courses and student teaching seminars. The book is also useful as a resource in professional development programs and community education programs, in which caring adults seek to improve their knowledge and skills for helping young people learn and grow.

The approach taken in this casebook is consistent with the trend in teacher education, in which teachers and prospective teachers are invited to become active inquirers in their work and in so doing, emphasize reflectivity, interaction, speculative thinking, contextual influence, and personal meaning making.

The cases in this collection are engaging, problem-based stories of authentic classroom situations. Because the situations are generic, they are relevant to teachers and prospective teachers in grades K–6 throughout the full range of subject matter areas.

Teaching in Today's Classrooms: Cases from Elementary School is based on this author's 21 years of teaching general and special methods courses for undergraduates and postbaccalaureate students, core courses on multicultural education, and student teaching seminars. The cases in the book have been field tested in these courses and further refined in the graduate continuing studies program for K–12 teachers in urban and suburban schools in the Minneapolis–St. Paul area, as well as in greater Minnesota.

Although case study methodology has become increasingly valued in teacher education as a way to develop teachers' ability to reflect and subsequently to behave in classrooms in ways that make a difference in students' lives (Morine-Dershimer, 1992), I wanted a set of cases that broadly represented and addressed the most important issues in teaching, that is, a set organized around a coherent, research-supported, conceptual framework. After examining a number of such models, I selected the "Framework for Teaching" by Charlotte Danielson (1996), a model based on PRAXIS III* Classroom Performance Assessments criteria developed by the Educational Testing Service, which acknowledges the need for developmentally appropriate

---

*The PRAXIS Series: Professional Assessments for Beginning Teachers is a research-based model comprising three components: PRAXIS I measures basic academic skills; PRAXIS II measures subject matter knowledge and pedagogy; and PRAXIS III focuses on classroom performance. For futher information contact Educational Testing Service, Princeton, NJ 08541.

practice, equity and inclusion, and high expectations. It features 22
critical components of teaching, organized within four domains:

I *Planning and preparation* for teaching in classrooms in
   which students engage in constructing meaning
II *Creating an environment for learning*, an environment of
   respect and rapport in which the teacher effectively manages
   materials, physical space, and student behavior
III *Instruction*, in which the teacher communicates clearly,
   engages students in learning, and provides quality feedback
IV *Professional responsibilities*, which includes working with
   students, parents, colleagues, and the community

Because the framework depends on context rather than prescribed behaviors, teachers can achieve excellence in diverse ways.
The components of the Danielson model correlate closely with the
Interstate New Teacher Assessment and Support Consortium (INTASC)
standards in teacher education (see Appendix A, Figure 2) and are
compatible with those of the National Board for Professional
Teaching Standards (NBPTS).

The first significant feature of this casebook, then, is that it is
organized around a coherent, broad-based, research-supported
framework, relevant for both preservice and inservice teachers.
From five to nine cases are provided to assist students in exploring
the critical components of teaching within each of the four domains.

Second, my students found that some of the previously published cases initially used in my classes were too lengthy and that the
extensive detail distracted them from the essential issues. Moreover,
they claimed that high levels of prescription often created a situation
that seemed too unique, too confusing, or simply too exhausting to
maintain a high level of attention. While there is a place for lengthy,
complex cases, there is also a need for more focused cases, such as
those in this collection. From the instructor's standpoint, the cases
can be used more flexibly—some may fit well in a shorter available
time period, while for longer periods, exploring a case in greater
depth or using two shorter cases might be desirable.

Third, as we enter the twenty-first century, it is crucial that
undergraduate and graduate teacher education programs and professional development programs in the nation's schools produce
school personnel with the knowledge, skills, and dispositions necessary for teaching students with diverse abilities, interests, and cultures. The cases in this collection encourage analysis of pedagogy
within a multicultural context.

Fourth, many other casebooks assign students a passive role in
terms of case design, that is, the cases were fully developed
without possibility for student input. This book offers instructors

and students the opportunity to develop the context within which a given case should be analyzed, so that students become involved in their own learning. Furthermore, at the end of each part, students are invited to create at least one case that could be shared with the class. Guidelines for constructing cases are provided.

Fifth, "Questions for Reflection" invite students to provide responses, collect further data, consider alternative perspectives, make decisions, and share their thoughts and feelings with others. "Activities for Extending Thinking" encourage students to think about cause/effect relationships; develop and use categories of knowledge, skills, and dispositions; and build and evaluate new paradigms and models. Both features invite students to relate insights to the course text, to field experiences or clinicals, and to national and local standards in teacher education.

Last, an extensive bibliography is offered as a bridge to the knowledge base. Selected bibliographies related to each of the four domains listed earlier are provided at the end of each part of the book. In addition, a list of relevant general references is provided at the end of the text itself.

Format

This casebook provides the student with real-life problems in a highly readable format, and the instructor with a research-based structure from which it is easy to teach. The book consists of five major sections. Part 1 provides an introduction with suggestions for analyzing and discussing the cases. Each of Parts 2 through 5 consists of cases representing components of one of Danielson's four domains (listed earlier). Each case

Begins with a brief overview (annotation)

Provides a concise story containing a pedagogical problem in a multicultural context

Offers "Questions for Reflection" followed by "Activities for Extending Thinking"

At the end of Parts 2 through 5, a selected bibliography of resources is provided.

An appendix contains Danielson's (1966) conceptual framework, including the four domains, 22 critical components of teaching, and correlations to INTASC standards, as well as an abbreviated version of the Banks (1997) model for integrating multicultural content into curriculum, a bibliography, and lists of references and reviews.

An *Instructor's Manual* is available to support instructors using the casebook. The *Instructor's Manual* contains suggestions for preparing for case analysis and organizing class discussion. It also features for each case a list of representative "Anticipated Responses" from field tests to help instructors anticipate student responses to the questions following that case.

I invite you to select and use the cases pertinent to your courses. The extent to which you employ case-based/problem-based learning can provide, on one hand, worthwhile enrichment of current courses, or on the other, nothing less than a route to major reform in your teacher education program.

Related Resources

Two other casebooks are available in this series, *A Casebook for Exploring Diversity in K–12 Classrooms* and *Teaching in Today's Classrooms: Cases from Middle and Secondary School.* Although some of the cases in these books may describe situations similar to those in this casebook, it should be noted that the primary focus of the "Questions for Reflection" in this casebook is on pedagogy for the elementary school, rather than issues of diversity or secondary education. In short, the same general case situation can be used in different classes as long as the focus of study remains on issues related to respective course goals.

Acknowledgments

For their ongoing love and support, not only in the writing of this casebook, but in all my efforts, I thank my family, Shari, Ryan, Angie, and daughter-in-law Stacy. Each truly has been a blessing in my life.

Others who contributed to the book include Dr. Eugene Anderson, professor of education, University of Minnesota. His mentorship in ways of thinking about education and teacher education has been invaluable. I have deeply valued his friendship, guidance, and support over the years. His suggestions regarding the organization and overall readability of this book have been most appreciated.

I thank Dr. Charles Bruning, professor of education (retired), close friend, and mentor. His wise counsel regarding the content of this book and his positive spirit have been encouraging indeed.

I thank, too, Charlotte Danielson, who so generously allowed the use of her "framework for teaching" as the basis for organizing the cases in this casebook.

For her analysis of case study format, validity and integrity of concepts, and multicultural sensitivity, I thank Dr. Darcia Narváez, Department of Curriculum and Instruction, University of Minnesota. Her work significantly strengthened the conceptual/theoretical aspects of the cases.

I also thank the many K–12 teachers, undergraduate and graduate students, and professors in teacher education and who reviewed the cases. Their assessment of the degree of clarity and realism of each of the cases helped greatly in confirming their potential for wider use. In particular, I thank the reviewers, Beatrice S. Fennimore, Indiana University of Pennsylvania; Margaret M. Ferrara, Central Connecticut State University; and Scott Hewit, Rollins College. I especially wish to thank Bonnie Houseman, ESL teacher candidate, Jon Halpern and Jeff Fink, veteran elementary teachers; and Ann Mabbott, director of Second Language Teaching and Learning at Hamline, for their valuable contributions.

Debbie Stollenwerk, senior editor, Prentice Hall, and JaNoel Lowe of Custom Editorial Productions have done a superb job in establishing a comfortable working relationship for creating and writing. I appreciate the guidance they have so generously provided.

For preparing the manuscript, I thank Wayne Gannaway, Pat Burt, Kate Touhey, and Julie Miller, all of Hamline University. Wayne and Pat persevered in making the numerous revisions necessary in the production of the manuscript, and Kate and Julie made valuable editorial suggestions. I also thank Leslie Kunze for her work in preparing the manuscript for the *Instructor's Manual*.

Last, without the encouragement and support of my colleagues at Hamline University, completion of this casebook would not have been possible. My sincere thanks to faculty in the Education Department—Colleen Bell, Jim Bonilla, Steve Jongewaard, Sandy Tutwiler, Dwight Watson, and Pat Werner—and to the faculty of the college as a whole.

G.L.R.

References

Banks, J., & Banks, C.A.M. (Eds.). (1997). *Multicultural education: Issues and perspectives.* Needham Heights, MA: Allyn & Bacon.

Danielson, C. (1996). *Enhancing professional practice: A framework for teaching.* Alexandria, VA: Association for Supervision and Curriculum Development.

Morine-Dershimer, G. (1992). *Patterns of interactive thinking associated with alternative perspectives on teacher planning.* Paper presented at the annual meeting of the American Association of Educational Researchers, San Francisco.

Redman, G.L. (1999). *A casebook for exploring diversity in K–12 classrooms..* Upper Saddle River, NJ: Merrill/Prentice Hall.

Redman, G.L. (1999). *Teaching in Today's Classrooms: Cases from middle and secondary school.* Upper Saddle River, NJ: Merrill/Prentice Hall.

About the Author

George Redman has taught in the public schools for 7 years, including 4 years in the Los Angeles area and 3 in an urban school in Minneapolis. He has also taught 21 years in the undergraduate teacher education program at Hamline University, in urban St. Paul, Minnesota; has served in Hamline's graduate and continuing studies program for teachers for more than 15 years; and has conducted numerous in-service professional development workshops and courses for K–12 teachers.

Dr. Redman's undergraduate responsibility has primarily been for three courses: Teaching in the Secondary School, a general methods course; Education and Cultural Diversity, a core course in the program; and Student Teaching. He has also taught courses entitled City as Classroom, Introduction to Microcomputers, and Self and Other. He has served as chair of the department for more than 10 years.

Dr. Redman is a past recipient of the Association of Teacher Educators (ATE) national award for outstanding research, and he has published numerous articles in professional journals. His Merrill books include *A Casebook for Exploring Diversity in K–12 Classrooms* and *Teaching in Today's Classrooms: Cases from the Middle and Secondary School*. He is co-author of *Self-Esteem for Tots to Teens,* and author of *Building Self-Esteem in Students: A Skill and Strategy Workbook for Teachers,* and *Building Self-Esteem in Children: A Skill and Strategy Workbook for Parents.*

Contents

Part I
Introduction

The Cases in This Casebook

The cases in this collection describe actual teaching/learning events that occur frequently in elementary classrooms. Although they are intended to be brief and easy to read, field tests indicate that the cases meet the criteria described by McNergney, Herbert, and Ford (1994); that is, they allow for "multiple levels of analysis [and] are sufficiently rich to make room for multiple interpretations" (p. 340).

Each case focuses on at least one "methodology" issue within one of four domains: (1) planning and preparation, (2) the classroom environment, (3) instruction, or (4) professional responsibilities (Danielson, 1996). The four domains contain a total of 22 of the most critical components of teaching (see Appendix A). Each case can stimulate thinking about more than one component of teaching and/or more than one issue, depending on the orientation of a given course or seminar and on the needs and interests of students. For example, in one of the cases, a teacher is asked by several students if they may focus their project on the contributions of a famous Native American chief rather than on one of the presidents on Mount Rushmore as originally assigned. In analyzing this case, your instructor may ask that you focus exclusively on methodological components of teaching, that is, responding to student needs and interests; or using a project-based approach in teaching; and/or examining in greater depth issues of cultural diversity, such as Native American views of U.S. presidents. Your analysis may include exploration of facts, concepts, or values. In short, each case is sufficiently rich to allow analysis of multiple issues, multiple levels of analysis, and multiple interpretations.

A unique feature of this book allows you to shape the context of each case to make it more personally relevant to the situation in which you are currently involved (e.g., a field experience) or in which you might be teaching. Guidelines for creating such context are provided. Your instructor will help determine the extent to which you will use this particular feature.

Cases and the Knowledge Base in Teacher Education

Case-based instruction is supported by the portion of the knowledge base that asserts that teacher's knowledge (1) is situation-specific (contextual), (2) is informed and informing through interaction (interactive), and (3) involves uncertainty (is speculative) (Clark & Lambert, 1986). Cases, then, provide situation-specific circumstances that can help you connect theory with practice in a supportive, interactive environment.

Schon (1987) has reported that teachers acquire the bulk of their professional knowledge through continuous action and reflection on everyday problems. Cases provide a point of departure for reflecting on those problems, and thus they help you create meaning from authentic teaching/learning situations.

A growing research base suggests varied benefits from such reflection. Adults who reflect on critical issues are said to

> develop the power to reason (Sprinthall & Thies-Sprinthall, 1983), enhance their cognitive complexity (Hunt & Sullivan, 1974; Oja & Sprinthall, 1978), perceive meaningfulness (Kennedy, 1991), alter their belief structure (Peterson, Carpenter, & Tennema, 1989), and think like professionals (Kleinfeld, 1992; Morine-Dershimer, 1991). Although further research on case-method teaching is needed, interest is growing in its use to encourage the development of such reflective action (McNergney, Herbert, & Ford, 1994).

The Benefits of Cases

Cases provide an opportunity for prospective and practicing teachers to address real problems; to retrieve principles of teaching and learning to resolve those problems; and to construct, share, and evaluate responses with others. More specifically, according to Merseth (1991), as cited in Cooper (1995), case methods

1. Help develop skills of critical analysis and problem solving, including skills of observing, making inferences, identifying relationships, and articulating organizing principles
2. Encourage reflective practice and deliberate action—they require students to discuss and choose from competing interpretations advanced by one another
3. Provide a context in which students can make decisions in complex situations when there is not an exact match between theory and practice
4. Involve students in their own learning—active responsibility takes the place of passive acceptance that might exist in a lecture situation
5. Encourage the development of a community of learners by/through lively and engaging discussion and collaborative teamwork

Developing such healthy habits of the mind prepares you for dealing with the real and perplexing problems you will face in teaching.

Cultural Diversity in Today's Schools

Cultural diversity is indeed a critical aspect of today's schools, and it must be seriously considered when studying methods of teaching. The key to understanding cultural diversity is in one's definition of *culture*. Although the term can be defined in various ways, the broad definition offered by Pusch (1979) best serves our discussion:

> Culture is the sum total of ways of living: including values, beliefs, aesthetic standards, linguistic expression, patterns of thinking, behavioral norms, and styles of communication which a group of people has developed to assure its suvival in a particular physical and human environment. (p. 3)

Cultural diversity does not simply refer to the existence of groups such as "poor," or "black," or "Jewish." Rather, the term as used herein considers every human group to be diverse. Even those in an all-white "college-prep" class are diverse in their values, beliefs, aesthetic standards, and ways of learning and living.

Teachers who respect and support cultural diversity, then, integrate into their teaching information on the values, beliefs, and other factors identified by Pusch (1979). Those teachers have as a primary goal the development in all students of an understanding of and appreciation for the human potential of persons of all backgrounds.

The approach to teaching and learning used by teachers to foster cultural diversity is often referred to as *multicultural education*. Bennett (1995) considers the four key components of multicultural education to be the movement toward equity, the multicultural curriculum approach, the process of becoming multicultural, and the commitment to combat prejudice and discrimination. Some suggest that when

> teachers examine the issues of ethics, morals, and justice in education, they . . . begin to question common practices such as tracking, ability grouping, competitive grading, and behavioral control. They begin ... to look for the hidden lessons about equity and power that might lie therein. (Sparks-Langer & Colton, 1991, p. 4.)

The study of teaching, then, is best done within the context of today's schools—schools that prepare students for life in a culturally diverse world. The cases in this book allow for examination of critical teaching/learning issues within a multicultural context.

Tips for Preparing for Discussion of a Case

The following steps are recommended in preparing for a case study discussion:

1. Read the case quickly for general understanding.
2. Further develop the cultural and educational context for the case. Suggestions for doing so are offered in the following section entitled "Creating Additional Context for the Cases." Your instructor may ask that this be done individually or in a group, and as an out-of-class or an in-class activity.
3. Reread the case, in light of the details that you added. Take notes on key issues and list questions that arise. Examine outside resources if time permits.
4. Answer the "Questions for Reflection" at the end of the case as well as any designed by your instructor, and complete the "Activities for Extending Thinking" assigned by your instructor.
5. Identify additional activities that might extend thinking on the issue(s) in the case. For example, if you are aware of a resource or a site that could be visited by classmates to expand or refine thinking about an issue, suggest it to your instructor.

Creating Additional Context for the Cases

Whereas it is important that each case centers on at least one of the 22 critical components of teaching (Danielson, 1996), it is likewise important that you have the opportunity to shape the contextual details of each case, for you bring to the case analysis both prior knowledge and personal purpose. In analyzing a case, you may draw ideas from, and apply insights to, a field experience or teaching assignment. More specifically, you are invited to add detail describing the community, school, and classroom in each of the cases you analyze. Your instructor will determine which cases need additional context and the amount of detail you should add. In some cases, for consistency, an instructor may have you analyze the story as written or may provide additional context for you.

Prior to the series of cases in Parts 2 to 5, you will find guidelines for listing additional community, school, and classroom factors that might make the case richer, more authentic, or more personally relevant. More specifically, you will be invited to list factors such as characteristics of the school and community (e.g., proportion of socioeconomic, ethnic, and religious groups) and the nature of the individuals and the classroom in the case (e.g., personal characteristics, type of curriculum).

You may also find it helpful to review the information in Appendix C on national estimates of various ethnic groups, children in poverty, exceptionality, and affectional orientation. Limit the number of details that you add to a given case—perhaps to four or five—so that the key issues in the case are not lost.

To further encourage your active participation in the learning process, at the end of each of the four major sections of cases, you will be invited to design a case study of your own. A form with guidelines is provided (e.g., see pp. 34–35).

Participating in Class Discussions

Participation in class discussions of case studies should take place in the spirit of cooperation. Whether discussion occurs in large or small groups, your learning will be maximized if everyone has an equal opportunity to support one another's learning.

I encourage participants to employ good listening skills such as those described in Anderson, Redman, and Rogers (1991) and Redman (1992), including paraphrasing, empathizing, asking open questions, asking clarifying questions (e.g., "Do we really know that?"), and nonverbal attending (smiling, nodding, and the like). Destructive criticism, ridicule, interrupting, and similar rejecting behaviors should be avoided.

Finally, it is recommended that you record and share insights on *changes* in (1) particular ideas and (2) the patterns of the responses as the discussion progresses. For example, in a given case, you or a classmate may have initially taken the view of the teacher (either a particular idea or a general approach) but through discussion may come to support the student perspective. Your instructor may ask that these insights be recorded in writing and submitted to her or him.

Conclusion

Be assured that the cases you are about to examine represent real problems related to the most critical components of teaching in today's elementary schools—components grounded in sound research and an extensive knowledge base (Danielson, 1996).

I invite you to be creative as you create case contexts, explore issues of methodology and diversity, relate them to field experiences and to research and/or teaching experiences, and design cases of your own. The process of thoroughly examining and discussing authentic classroom problems helps good teachers learn and grow and become even better—it is the epitome of professional development. Enjoy!

References

Anderson, E. M., Redman, G. L., & Rogers, C. (1991). *Self-esteem for tots to teens.* Wayzata, MN: Parenting and Teaching Publications.

Banks, J. A. (1994). *An introduction to multicultural education.* Boston: Allyn & Bacon.

Bennett, C. (1995). *Comprehensive multicultural education: Theory and practice* (3rd ed.). Needham Heights, MA: Allyn & Bacon.

Clark, C., & Lampert, M. (1986). The study of teacher thinking: Implications for teacher education. *Journal of Teacher Education, 37,* 27-31.

Cooper, J. (Ed.). (1995). *Teachers' problem-solving: A casebook of award-winning teaching cases.* Needham Heights, MA: Allyn & Bacon.

Danielson, C. (1996). *Enhancing professional practice: A framework for teaching.* Alexandria, VA: Association for Supervision and Curriculum Development.

Hunt, D. E. & Sullivan, E. V. (1974). *Between psychology and education.* New York: Holt, Rinehart and Winston.

Kennedy, M. M. (1991). *An agenda for research on teacher learning. (Special Report).* East Lansing, MI: National Center for Research on Teacher Learning.

Kleinfield, J. (1992). Learning to think like a teacher: The study of cases. In J. H. Schulman (Ed.), *Case methods in teacher education* (pp. 33-49). New York: Teachers College Press.

McNergney, R., Herbert, J., & Ford, R. (1993, March). *Anatomy of a team case competition.* Paper presented at the annual meeting of the American Educational Research Association, Washington, DC.

McNergney, R., Herbert, J., & Ford, R. (1994). Cooperation and competition in case-based education. *Journal of Teacher Education, 45*(5), 339-345.

Merseth, K. K. (1991). *The case for cases in teacher education.* Washington, DC: American Association for Higher Education and the American Association of Colleges for Teacher Education.

Morine-Dershimer, G. (1991). Learning to think like a teacher. *Teaching and Teacher Education, 7*(2), 159-168.

Oja, S., & Sprinthall, N. A. (1978). Psychological and moral development for teachers. In N. A. Sprinthall & R. L. Mosher (Eds.), *Value development as the aim of education* (pp. 117-134). Schenectady, NY: Charter Press.

Peterson, P. L., Carpenter, T., & Fennema, E. (1989). Teacher's knowledge of student's knowledge in mathematics problem solving: Correlational and case analysis. *Journal of Educational Psychology, 81,* 558-569.

Pusch, M.D. (Ed.). (1979). *Multicultural education: A cross-cultural training approach.* Yarmouth, ME: Intercultural Press.

Redman, G. L. (1992). *Building self-esteem in students: A skill and strategy workbook for teachers.* Wayzata, MN: Parenting and Teaching Publications.

Schon, D. A. (1987). *Educating the reflective practitioner.* San Fransisco: Jossey-Bass.

Schulman, L. (1992). Toward a pedagogy of cases. In J. H. Shulman, *Case methods in teacher education* (pp. 1-32). New York: Teachers College Press.

Sparks-Langer, G. M., & Colton, A. B. (1991, March). Synthesis of research on teacher reflective thinking. *Educational Leadership, 48*(6), 37-44.

Sprinthall, N. A. & Thies-Sprinthall, L. (1983). The teacher as an adult learner: A cognitive-developmental view. *National Society for the Study of Education Yearbook (Pt.2),* 13-35.

Part 2
Planning and Preparation

Creating Additional Context for a Given Case

Each case in this section is sufficiently complex to allow for multiple levels of analysis and multiple interpretations. Even so, it is important to bring your own knowledge and personal purpose to the analysis of a given case. Hence, the context within each case has purposely not been highly prescribed. For example, most of the cases purposely do not indicate the grade level, thereby allowing for a variety of readers to bring their own grade-level context to the case.

Therefore, as suggested in the introduction, prior to analyzing a given case, you are invited to modify its context. Your instructor will help decide which cases might be modified and the extent of the modifications and will direct you to do so individually, in small groups, or as a class.

When so directed by your instructor, include factors that make the case richer, more authentic, or more personally meaningful to you, your small group, or your class. You may want to re-create a context that resembles a school in which you are currently completing a field experience or in which you are teaching, or you may want to create a setting representing the type of school that you hope to work in some day. Include one or two factors from the following categories:

Characteristics of the community. You might include such factors as proportion of socioeconomic, ethnic, and religious groups and the sociopolitical attitudes of various community groups.

Characteristics of the school. You might include demographics related to the ethnic, religious, and special needs make-up of the student body; curricular and extracurricular emphases of the school; and recent school reform efforts.

Nature of the characters and the classroom. You might include information such as personal characteristics (e.g., physical appearance, social abilities, mannerisms and behavioral habits, intellectual abilities, and teaching or learning styles) or grade level of the class, physical arrangement of the classroom, type of curriculum, and daily schedule of the classes.

For those cases identified by your instructor for analysis and for context modification, take a few minutes prior to analysis to list in writing several additional contextual variables that you believe are important.

Case I

An experience with a new student reminds a teacher to use
caution in relating socioeconomic status to outward appearance.

But I Assumed. . .

Mr. McDonald was a new teacher at Lincoln School, located in an economically deprived neighborhood. He was a strong believer in teaching the whole child, in active learning, and in multicultural education.

It was the sixth week of school when Peter, an African American transfer student from Chicago, entered his class. Mr. McDonald welcomed Peter into the class and gave him handouts related to the current unit and a set of free lunch tickets for the remainder of the week.

"Any questions?" asked Mr. McDonald.

"Well, just one," Peter said. "What do I do with these tickets?"

"Just give them to the woman at the cash register in the lunchroom," replied Mr. McDonald. He then began his geography lesson.

Later in the hour, when he was well into his lesson, Mr. McDonald asked, "Can anyone tell me if one could get to Europe via the North Sea?"

"Yes," Peter replied. "I've crossed the North Sea by boat on a trip to Europe."

Doubting that Peter had ever made such a trip, Mr. McDonald replied, "You're right, Peter; it is possible to reach Europe by the North Sea." As the hour was coming to an end, Mr. McDonald reminded students of the homework for the next day. Just as the dismissal bell rang, he finished giving the assignments.

On the way out, Robert, a slight boy, stopped by Mr. McDonald, who was standing at the door. In the past few days, the boy had become a bit more "clingy." He also seemed to have more difficulty sitting still—he would slide back and forth in his seat as if to scratch himself. "See you tomorrow, Robert," said Mr. McDonald. Robert smiled and disappeared in a sea of faces.

On his way out of the room, Peter asked Mr. McDonald where he should go to get a bus pass. Mr. McDonald informed Peter that he would not need one—that all the kids walked home. Peter glanced quizzically at his new teacher and then was swallowed by the stream of students.

The next morning when Mr. McDonald made his usual stop in the principal's office to get his announcements and messages, the school secretary reminded him to have Peter pick up his bus pass. Mr. McDonald admitted that he had told Peter to walk home the day before.

"Five miles!?" asked the secretary. "You know he was adopted by a family living in Roseville, don't you?"

Mr. McDonald admitted that he had not known that Peter was a member of a transracial family living in a neighboring middle-class community. "That explains Peter's puzzled look when I handed him the free lunch tickets," he thought. Mr. McDonald wondered what he would say to Peter later that day in class.

Questions for Reflection

1. What were Mr. McDonald's assumptions about Peter and on what did he base them?
2. In your experience as a student, what assumptions have teachers made about you because of your ethnicity, gender, socioeconomic status, or other cultural attributes? Briefly describe one or two incidents.
3. What should teachers do to avoid the kinds of problems in this story? Where possible, should teachers use cumulative files to learn about students?
4. If you were Mr. McDonald, what would you say to Peter in class later that day?
5. What hypotheses might you suggest for Robert's behavior? What, if anything, would you do about it?

Activities for Extending Thinking

1. Talk with at least three students of varying cultural backgrounds whom you do not know well. Discuss with each student his or her likes and dislikes with respect to out-of-class activities (e.g., hobbies, pets), as a way to get to know more about his or her cultural heritage, interests, skills, emotional needs, and approaches to learning. Be prepared to summarize your insights in class.
2. Review one research-based resource from the "Suggested Readings" at the end of this part that relates to the issue of getting to know students. Summarize key insights in writing and be prepared to share in class.

Case 2

*Students from an economically deprived neighborhood
are given a writing assignment in which they express their
feelings about the hurtful effects of gang activity.*

My Brother Was Shot by a Gang*

Ms. Soltow was well liked by her students and colleagues. She was fully aware that many of her students were from homes ravaged by crime and poverty. Gang activity was commonplace. Many students had one parent at home—in most cases, a mother. Many of her students had to work at home, baby-sitting, for example, to help their working parent or parents. Many of the students, though only 12 years old, had lost friends or relatives to homicide.

In an attempt to meet some of the emotional needs of her students, and at the same time provide an opportunity for them to develop their writing abilities, Ms. Soltow addressed the class: "Often in life we are hurt by others—others who don't mean to hurt us, but nevertheless do. Can anyone give an example of how someone has hurt you?"

Raymond replied: "My brother. He's been shot twice and still hangs with a gang. It hurts me when he gets injured."

Ms. Soltow could see the pain on Raymond's face; tears had come to his eyes. "That's a good example of how we can be hurt by someone who doesn't mean to hurt us. I can see why that would cause pain. Does anyone else have a story to share?" she asked so as to give Raymond time to wipe his eyes. Several other students told similar stories.

Ms. Soltow redirected her attention to the rest of the class: "I'd like each of you to take out a sheet of paper and write about how someone has hurt you even though they didn't mean to. Be sure you state exactly how you felt at the time and how you feel about it now. I'll come around and help those who might like some assistance. Are there any questions before we start?"

For approximately 15 minutes the students wrote and Ms. Soltow circulated, encouraging them to think further about their

---

*Based on an idea portrayed in Shapiro, A. (Executive Producer), & Fleisher, C. L. (Writer, Producer, & Director). *The Truth About Teachers* [Videotape]. (Available from Pyramid Film and Video, 2801 Colorado Avenue, Santa Monica, CA 90404).

feelings and then to express them in writing. She provided time for volunteers to share what they could about their painful experiences. Finally, she provided a list of criteria for judging the prewriting samples and allowed the remaining 15 minutes for students to evaluate their writing on the criteria distributed.

Questions for Reflection

1. Assess Ms. Soltow's strategy of having students write about how they had been hurt by someone. Was it suitable for her students, considering their age and backgrounds and her instructional goals? What else could she have done? What should she have done instead?
2. Assess her response to Raymond. What would you have done differently? What else would you have done to follow up with Raymond?
3. To what degree should teachers integrate students' personal feelings and personal lives outside of school into their instructional goals?
4. In addition to student needs and the nature of the discipline (e.g., English), what other factors must a teacher take into account when selecting instructional goals?

Activity for Extending Thinking

1. Discuss with at least one teacher, one curriculum coordinator, and one parent those factors they believe should be considered when designing/selecting instructional goals for diverse students. Be prepared to summarize your findings in class.

Case 3

A teacher considers ways in which she can integrate computer technologies with cultural and individual preferences to meet the academic and socioemotional needs of her students more effectively.

Our Computer Exercises Aren't Fun!

Ms. Wright was pleased that for each of the past five years the school had significantly increased the number of computers and software programs available to students. She also believed that neither computers nor software were culturally neutral, that they reflected the assumptions, expectations, and learning styles of their creators, and so she constantly looked for ways to integrate computer culture with the culture of individual students and the classroom.

To improve cross-cultural skills and intercultural understanding, Ms. Wright had worked hard to develop an ongoing activity in which each student identified and communicated with a pen pal from another country. She was pleased that the students were enthusiastic about using telecommunications technology to learn about the beliefs, behaviors, and values of persons of other cultures.

In activities involving research on the Internet, Ms. Wright encouraged multidirectional learning. She was as eager to learn from students as she was to have them learn from her, and she encouraged students to help one another whenever possible.

Ms. Wright made every attempt to use computer technology flexibly as a means to support a variety of individual and cultural differences. For example, she used visual and graphic representations preferred by some Native American students as a way of understanding; she established pairs and trios at computers as a way to meet the preference for cooperative learning of many African, Asian, and Hispanic students; and she provided an overview and review of material, thereby adding a more global, less fragmented view preferred by many of her culturally diverse students.

In each of her classes, Ms. Wright had several students with limited English proficiency (LEP). These students were of Russian, Croatian, and Puerto Rican heritage. Although her LEP students were bright, their limited English proficiency kept them a bit behind the other students in learning subject matter content. In order to attend to their need to learn English, Ms. Wright would often allocate the last 15 minutes of class for the LEP students to use the computers to complete drill and practice programs on English grammar, usage, and punctuation. During this same time, non-LEP students would engage in enrichment computer programs requiring creative problem solving. Ms. Wright believed that this was the best way to attend to the particular needs of both groups of students.

By the fifth week of the term, Juan and Vicki, two of her LEP students, had politely reported that the grammar and usage worksheets on the computer were "boring." "We are learning some English, I guess," said Juan. "But I get tired of doing the same thing almost every day."

Ms. Wright replied: "I think that using technology to help me meet the differing needs of two groups of students is effective and efficient. This way I'm able to help you as well as the other students at the same time."

Juan and Vicki appeared unconvinced. "It's boring," Vicki reiterated.

Questions for Reflection

1. What do you consider to be the strengths of Ms. Wright's approach to integrating computer culture with individual student and classroom culture?
2. What would you change about her approach?
3. Identify your philosophical/theoretical approach to teaching (e.g., developmentalist, interactionist, behaviorist, experiential, or problem-based). Give an example of how you would design a coherent unit based on the approach you have identified; that is, describe the logic you would use in choosing and sequencing learning activities within that instructional unit. (A general outline of a unit will suffice.)

Activities for Extending Thinking

1. Interview an experienced teacher about his or her strategies for designing coherent instructional units. Include issues such as central philosophical or theoretical approach, rationale for choosing and for sequencing activities, and achieving integration across disciplines (e.g., development of thematic units). Be prepared to share insights from your interview in class.
2. Review a piece of software designed for student use. Identify its effectiveness as a tool for culturally and linguistically diverse students.
3. Interview a computer resource teacher and discuss content-specific software that will enhance the learning of English by LEP students. Create a list of these software items.

Case 4

A teacher and principal discuss programs and resources for two Hispanic students, each of whom has a learning disability and limited language proficiency.

Students With Dual Needs

Ms. Perez was regarded by students and colleagues as a hard-working and well-respected third grade teacher at Central. She loved children and wanted them to enjoy learning. She was warm and compassionate, had a good sense of humor, and, at the same time, was clearly in charge of her classroom. She acted quickly and fairly when her young students needed guidance or correction. She spoke both English and Spanish fluently.

Ms. Perez was committed to designing lessons that were developmentally appropriate and that reflected the culturally diverse society in which her students were likely to live. She learned quickly about the characteristics, needs, interests, and abilities of her students. Although she admitted to not having extensive knowledge about the many ethnicities, special abilities, and language acquisition needs of children, she worked hard at identifying resources that might supplement her knowledge.

Two of Ms. Perez's Hispanic students, Rita and Ramona, now in their third year in an English-speaking school, possessed highly developed oral language skills in both English and Spanish, and a learning disability resulting in limited reading and writing abilities. Ms. Perez had made certain that the learning disability had been properly diagnosed, for she knew that academic English takes much longer to develop than oral English and that sometimes educators *assume* that the problem is a learning disability. Both girls had been similarly diagnosed in the Spanish-speaking school they had attended before coming to Central.

Ms. Perez aggressively supported a more holistic, student-centered collaborative approach in which the girls would be placed in a general education setting, experience an oral-based bilingual curriculum, and work on developing reading and writing skills in the content areas. Ms. Perez contacted special service program personnel in bilingual and ESL programs, special education, and counseling and worked with friends and colleagues to identify bilingual community members who could tutor the girls after school. She was indeed an advocate for the culturally and linguistically diverse (CLD) students in her room.

Ms. Perez was in the fourth month of school when she had an idea that might improve an important resource. One day during lunch break, she encountered Ms. Williams, the principal, in the cafeteria. "Ms. Williams, I was wondering if it would benefit our staff and students if we were to offer some parent training programs that would help the parents become better at working with their children in reading, writing, and speaking," began Ms. Perez. "We could focus on practical interaction skills for building self-esteem and on positive approaches to managing child behavior. What do you think?"

"Sounds like a great idea!" replied Ms. Williams. "Mr. Lopez would have a lot to offer in the area of self-esteem, and we could identify other Latino role models as speakers. We could also see if those who come to the first session or two would want to establish support groups—perhaps neighborhood based—to conduct ongoing discussions of our sessions and of personally relevant problems. I think it could work!"

"I think so too," said Ms. Perez. "And perhaps later on there will be opportunities to encourage parent input on making curriculum more culturally relevant. It might be one good way of empowering parents."

"Let's bring it up at the next faculty meeting and see what we can do to move ahead. I'm all for it!" said Ms. Williams. She continued, "On a related topic, I've been wondering if Rita and Ramona should be moved to a self-contained classroom for learning disabled students. They would be with students with similar needs and the instruction would be in English, the language in which they need the most work. What do you think?"

Ms. Perez had always thought that the current general education arrangement was the best for the two girls. At the same time, on other issues, she had usually agreed with Ms. Williams, whom she considered to be a wise administrator. Perhaps moving the girls from their current general education program into the special education class could have significant benefits for them.

Questions for Reflection

1. What initial thoughts and feelings do you have in response to Ms. Perez's dilemma about a general versus special education placement for Rita and Ramona?
2. How would you respond to the principal regarding her proposal to move the girls to a self-contained special education classroom? Provide a rationale for your response.
3. What other school and community resources *for teachers* would be helpful in dealing with CLD students?

4. What other school and community resources *for students* would be helpful in dealing with CLD students?
5. What suggestions would you have for modifying or expanding Ms. Perez's plan for a parent education program?

Activities for Extending Thinking

1. Identify specific school and community resources available to a school in your area (perhaps a school in which you are currently involved in a field experience, or in which you are teaching) for (a) all students and (b) students of traditionally underrepresented groups.
2. Identify parent education programs in a local school (perhaps a school in which you are in a field experience or in which you are teaching). Briefly describe their goals, methods, and evidence of progress toward those goals.
3. Identify and interpret legal aspects of bilingual and special education, including major civil rights legislation, the Bilingual Education Act (also known as Title VII), the Individuals with Disabilities Education Act of 1990, and related case law.
4. On the Internet, explore state resources (e.g., state departments of education) and national resources (e.g., U.S. Department of Education—http://www.ed.gov/index.html)for curriculum planning in the future. Develop a list of other sites, such as Administration for Children and Families—http://www.acf. dhhs.gov/ and Children Now—http://www.dnai.com/~children/
Explore other such general sites as well as those more specific to instruction of CLD students.
5. Participate in an education listserv and/or newsgroup such as that at http://edweb.cnidr.org:90/usenets.html
Keep a journal of your participation.
6. Interview a parent of a CLD student to ascertain his or her views on how the school can provide services for his or her child.
7. Contact a community agency that works with CLD, ESL, or bilingual students to learn what programs are available for children and parents.

Case 5

A teacher designs a math lesson that not only teaches graphing but also helps raise student awareness of social issues.

When Would I Ever Use This?

Ms. McMullen had taught fifth grade for five years. She was a competent teacher. One of her favorite subjects was math. She had kept up with of developments in the field, including the use of manipulatives to help students engage in concrete activities. Moreover, she could really see that students were learning the content of the subject, and she knew it would be important in their lives as students in school and beyond.

Ms. McMullen had noticed a recent news report on a poll on perceptions of whites and blacks about the economic conditions of blacks in America. As she began planning for her next unit on constructing and interpreting charts and graphs, she decided that by using the current data from the article, she could not only teach math (graphing), but she could also teach a lesson on race relations.

On the first day of her unit, Ms. McMullen introduced the academic objectives of the math unit, defined some key terms, and outlined the benefits of understanding the charts and graphs. She showed how to represent data in a bar graph, a line graph, and a pie chart.

She then assigned students the task of reading and summarizing the material from a recent study on racial attitudes that was conducted by a major newspaper, a well-known foundation, and a reputable Ivy League university. Finally, she informed students that they should present the data in the form of a graph. They could follow any of the charts or graphs she had introduced, but they had to be able to defend their choice. She was curious to hear the rationales they would give.

In their graphs, students were to represent the subjects in the survey sample in terms of ethnicity and to depict what they considered to be key findings of the survey, for example, that 68 percent of blacks surveyed said that racism is a big problem in our society today, whereas only 38 percent of whites thought so; and 46 percent of whites said that blacks on average hold jobs of equal quality to those of whites, whereas government data show that blacks on average earn 60 percent less than whites.

Ms. McMullen planned to focus first on the mathematical aspects of the lesson and then later connect those ideas with the issues surrounding the racial attitude aspects of the activity.

Questions for Reflection

1. Is Ms. McMullen's notion of connecting two lessons (graphing and race relations) consistent with accepted views of best practice? Would you support her efforts to integrate the two lessons? Why or why not?
2. Would the cultural make-up of the class, for example, all white students, or a majority of students of color, affect your answer to question 1?
3. Have you ever taught a lesson in which you connected some "traditional" subject matter such as graphing, reading, writing, or computing with issues of social justice? Describe the lesson briefly. Describe how students responded to the lesson. If you have not taught such a lesson, speculate on how you could teach some traditional subject matter content along with issues of social justice (e.g., race relations, gender equity).
4. List the disciplines that you teach. Identify pedagogical techniques particular to each discipline (e.g., teaching science through inquiry or laboratory-based techniques). Be prepared to share your list in class.

Activity for Extending Thinking

1. Interview at least two practicing teachers about how they ensure that their lessons are aligned with students' cultural and developmental needs and interests. Be prepared to summarize your findings in class.

Case 6

By employing a number of special instructional strategies, a teacher tries to ensure that students with learning disabilities will succeed.

Structuring for Success in a Mainstreamed Classroom

Mr. French believed that mainstreaming students with mental and physical disabilities would benefit not only those with the disability, but the nondisabled as well. Over the past four years, he had given much thought to how best to arrange his instruction to ensure that both groups of students would learn. For example, for the disabled students, he regularly limited problems so that they focused their learning on a single concept; he included in assignments only material that was essential to the task at hand; and he collected student work as soon as it was completed so that he could give immediate feedback. In addition, he held frequent, short, one-on-one conferences in which he asked the student to restate his or her responsibilities with respect to the assignment. Last, he had a corner of his room set aside for mainstreamed students so that they could work in a quiet, uncrowded area whenever they wanted. They frequently took advantage of this opportunity.

It was the first week of school, and Mr. French was planning his lesson for the next day. His goal was for students to learn a number of social skills that they could use in his, as well as in other, classes. He would begin with listening skills and question-asking skills, for these were two skill groups with students with which learning disability and attention deficit/hyperactivity disorder, not to mention students with other disabilities and students with no disabilities, often had trouble.

He would have students work in groups of five. Since there were five students with learning disabilities in his class this term, they could form one group. Mr. French reasoned that having them work together would give each student a sense of support, knowing that each of them had a learning disability and no one would make fun of them.

Once the groups were formed, he would briefly define and model one of the four good listening skills: paraphrasing, empathizing, asking open questions, and asking clarifying questions, and then allow them to practice each skill, through role play. If he modeled one at a time, students would be able to focus on that skill and not be confused with too many new concepts at once. After the groups were finished practicing the skills, the class as a large group would discuss the effects of the role play (e.g., was it easier or harder than they had expected to use the skills; what problems did they have; what seemed to work well?).

Each previous year, the students had seemed to enjoy the role play activity. Mr. French always believed that students had achieved their goals in the activity.

Questions for Reflection

1. Which of the learning activities used by Mr. French would you support as consistent with his goal of maximizing learning for both the disabled and nondisabled students? Why? Which would you consider not to be consistent in light of his goals? Why?
2. Was Mr. French's grouping strategy suitable for both disabled and nondisabled students? Give evidence from research to support your answer.
3. In his activity for teaching good listening skills, did the lesson progress logically (i.e., from knowing the skill, to guided practice in using the skill, to independent practice), as suggested by research? What other, logical progression, if any, would you suggest?
4. How can teachers organize the physical space in the classroom to facilitate learning? Consider factors such as arrangement of furniture, use of teaching aides (e.g., overheads, flip charts, computer presentation programs), and student accessibility to learning resources.

Activity for Extending Thinking

1. Discuss with at least two special education teachers pedagogical techniques appropriate for various types of special needs students. List grouping strategies, common sources of student error, and proven subject-based pedagogy for each kind of special need. In addition to identifying patterns of learning for each special needs group, identify individual differences within those patterns. Provide some demographic data on number of special education students in the school: number of males, females, students of color, and bilingual students, and the number of each group that have been mainstreamed.

Case 7

A bilingual teacher's aide ponders specific strategies for helping teachers better understand their ESL and bilingual students' abilities, interests, prior knowledge, and individual needs.

A Bilingual Teacher's Aide Assesses His New School

It was the first day of school and Andy Seng, a bilingual teacher's aide with 10 years of experience, entered his new school building. He was excited to meet the staff and students.

He had been pleased when he attended the workshop week prior to the first week of actual classes. He had seen "Welcome" signs in several different languages posted above the doors; had been greeted by bilingual volunteers, some of whom were students and some of whom were community members; and had noticed universal symbols and photos over important places, such as the bathrooms, cafeteria, library, and school office. He had also seen that many of the classrooms contained resource books in a number of different languages, and he had talked to teachers who said that they encouraged journal writing in the student's first language. All of these factors, he thought, would help to develop a positive atmosphere for English as a Second Language (ESL) and bilingual students.

He and the principal had decided during workshop week that it might be useful for him to shadow one or two ESL students during the first day to get an idea of school and classroom policies and practices relative to ESL and bilingual pupils. On his first day, he followed two Vietnamese students, one throughout the morning, the other during the afternoon. Both had been placed in a mainstreamed classroom taught only in English.

At the end of each half day, he spoke with each student. "How did you like your morning?" he asked the first student, whose name was Hung.

"It was confusing," Hung replied. "My teacher had the class work in small groups. Since I didn't know what to do, I just watched the other students. And later on the playground the teacher had us play softball. She thought we'd all know how, but I had never heard of softball before. I was embarrassed."

When Andy asked Chau, the student he followed during the afternoon, Chau responded, "I think my teacher thinks I'm not as smart as the others. He gave me problems that were much more simple than those he gave to the other students." Chau paused, "After class some of the kids made fun of the lunch I brought from home—that made me feel bad."

Andy had worked as a teacher's aide for five years in each of two other schools. He knew that most teachers accepted, appreciated, and supported ESL and bilingual students. However, he had also seen a few teachers who had expectations that were either much too low or much too high for such students. Most cases of too-high expectations involved students of Asian heritage; cases of too-low expectations often involved Latino or African American students. Based on his past experience, then, Chau's situation was an exception to the rule.

Andy thanked both Hung and Chau for their responses and promised both of them that he would support them and other ESL and bilingual students throughout the term.

After school that day, Andy pondered ways that he might help teachers know more about the abilities, interests, and needs of each of their ESL and bilingual students. He knew that just telling teachers in a memo or even personally would not necessarily result in their knowing students better. He knew his goal was to be an advocate for students; now he just had to identify the strategies.

Questions for Reflection

1. Andy noted some positive steps the school and some individual teachers had taken to make students from other cultures feel more at home. What were they? What else could the school have done to this end?
2. The students also mentioned some teacher behaviors that had a detrimental effect on student morale. What behaviors did they note? What would you have done differently in each case?

Teacher behaviors with detrimental effects	What I would have done
a.	
b.	
c.	

3. What kinds of information should teachers have about individual students? From what sources could they obtain each type of information?
4. Consider a similar episode involving two students of another culture or of two different cultures, for example, two Russian students, or a Muslim and a Jewish student, or a Native American and a Hispanic student. What cultural issues would likely be raised?

Activities for Extending Thinking

1. Discuss with officials of a local school the language diversity within that school. List the different languages spoken and services for students who speak them. Include bilingual, ESL, and limited English proficiency (LEP) services and programs.
2. Talk with a bilingual and an ESL teacher to identify strategies they use to get to know their bilingual, ESL, and LEP students.

Case 8

A teacher guides students in the exposing of myths that perpetuate stereotypes and in using writing and speaking as vehicles for change.

Developing Skills of Critical Analysis: Exposing the Myths of Films and Fairy Tales*

Ms. Christensen wanted her students to develop the tools necessary to critique every idea in terms of the degree to which it contributes to or distracts from the building of a just society. To this end, each year her class embarked on a journey of exploration of cartoons, children's movies, and stories.

This year she planned to begin with Ariel Dorfman's *The Empire's Old Clothes: What the Lone Ranger, Babar, and Other Innocent Heroes Do to Our Minds,* in which the author claims that both popular literature and children's literature function to perpetuate existing power structures and deny the possibility of greater equality.

Next, the class would critique cartoons and children's movies, including those with stars such as Bugs Bunny, Daffy Duck, Heckle and Jeckle, The Little Mermaid, Sleeping Beauty, Cinderella, Snow White, and Popeye, as the first step in dismantling old values and constructing more just ones. The class would identify the roles of people of color, as well as men and women in the films. They would look at the power relationships among the characters; listen for loaded words, such as "backward," "primitive," and "lazy"; and consider the effect of the story on the self-image of members of a diverse audience.

The final leg of the journey would involve students in sharing their critiques with audiences beyond the classroom. Such a step would suggest to students that their efforts were of larger import and indeed might lead to changes in their school, community, or state. Some students wrote a pamphlet to distribute to PTA members, while

*Credit for the idea on which this case is based is given to Christensen, L., (1994). Unlearning the myths that bind us. In *Rethinking our classrooms*, special edition of *Rethinking schools* (pp. 8-13). Milwaukee, WI: Rethinking Schools Limited.

others watched Saturday morning cartoons and wrote a report card for each ("Popeye" received an "F" because of its portrayal of ethnic groups as stupid and Americans as superior, and "Teenage Mutant Ninja Turtles" received a "D" because of its focus on using violence to solve problems).

Ms. Christensen noted that each year most students would look deeper into the issues and understood, for example, the master/servant relationship or how the images affected the dreams and goals of viewers or readers. A few, however, shrugged their shoulders and suggested that being rich or poor is OK, or that kids just read or view fairy tales as fun and do not really internalize the values portrayed. Ms. Christensen recalled occasional statements from students such as, "Just because girls see Tinkerbelle or Cinderella with tiny waists doesn't mean they'll want one." She wondered: "How can I determine how many of my students hold such beliefs and how firmly they hold them? How can I devise some valid, reliable, cost-effective ways to assess the degree to which my students are developing the knowledge, skills, and dispositions for thinking critically? What about performance and authentic assessment or portfolios?"

Questions for Reflection

1. What did you find effective about Ms. Christensen's use of literature and movies to teach values? What might you change?
2. How would you respond to the questions Ms. Christensen asked at the end of the story?
   a. How can she determine how many of her students believe that stereotypes in media are not harmful?
   b. How can she determine how firmly they hold this belief?
   c. How can she determine if students are improving in their ability to think critically as they participate in this unit of instruction? (Draw on knowledge about performance assessment, authentic assessment, and portfolios in responding to this question.)
3. Is it appropriate for teachers to challenge students' traditional social and role concepts, especially those based on family and religious values? If so, at what ages and under what conditions?
4. What goals regarding the teaching of traditional and nontraditional values would you select (design) for your classes?

Activity for Extending Thinking

1. Discuss with a parent, a teacher, and an administrator their philosophy about teaching values, particularly values embedded in

traditional fairy tales and children's literature. Discuss both the process (methods) of teaching values and the substance of the values themselves. Include the "Questions for Reflections" for this case in your discussions.

Case 9

A student who fails to turn in any assigned homework and contributes little to class, yet consistently gets the highest score on tests and quizzes, causes a teacher to rethink his system for assessing students.

How Should I Grade Danielle?

From the first day of the fall term, Danielle, an independent Latina student, had colored her nails with black marker and had worn long sweatshirts with names of hard-rock bands on the back. She had few friends but was generally friendly to those who approached her. In general, she was cordial, though somewhat distant, to her teacher, Mr. Edwards.

In class, Danielle rarely completed or turned in a homework assignment in any of her subject areas. She worked by herself when she could; when "forced" to work in a small group, she would tend to hold back and let other group members do the talking and the work. She never volunteered to answer any questions in class discussions. When Mr. Edwards would call on her, her answer would always be correct, but short. Moreover, she regularly had the highest quiz and test scores. In fact, on occasion she would get a perfect score, even on the larger, more difficult unit tests.

This combination of behaviors caused a problem for Mr. Edwards. Whereas his posted objectives usually required students to demonstrate understanding of concepts in homework assignments or small group discussions, his grading system had always put the vast majority of the weight on achievement as measured by tests. With this system, Danielle would easily earn a top grade (3) in each of her subjects. On the other hand, he wondered if Danielle's unwillingness to complete and turn in homework assignments and her reluctance to contribute to small groups and to class discussions should be factored into her grade. Certainly her behavior was not helpful in terms of modeling to other students the behaviors in which he would like them to engage, and the behaviors most of them needed in order to succeed.

To compound his problem, Mr. Edwards would always require self-evaluations at the end of each unit. Students were to assign to themselves a 1, 2, or 3, and to write a two-sentence rationale for the grade assigned. Mr. Edwards believed that, in general, it was most helpful to him to see how student self-evaluations compared to the grade he was about to assign based on scores in his grade book. Indeed, sometimes a discrepancy between the two would help him identify an error in his record keeping, perhaps a score that inadvertently he had not recorded. Danielle had again assigned herself a grade of 3 in each subject, using her high test scores as the basis for the grade.

Mr. Edwards, a second year teacher, often took such problems to his mentor teacher, Ms. Sundquist. Ms. Sundquist was in her ninth year as a successful teacher. "I think you need to be clear in your own mind about the outcomes you want for your students," advised Ms. Sundquist. "And then communicate the outcomes, standards, and criteria to your students."

"Well," replied Mr. Edwards, "is it legitimate to have as your goals such things as 'turns in homework' and 'contributes to small and large group discussions' and the like? If I have these as goals, then Danielle should perhaps get a 2 or 1. But when she has the highest test scores in the entire grade level, I'd have a hard time justifying that to her parents!"

"To be fair to students," asserted Ms. Sundquist, "the goals need to be meaningful and the students need to be clear about the criteria upon which their performance will be judged. For example, if asked to write a descriptive essay, they need to know if they will be assessed on organization, creativity, grammar and usage, spelling, punctuation, and/or other criteria. Some scholars recommend identifying levels of goal attainment, that is, "rubrics" on each of the standards, for example, for organization—what type of response would earn a high grade, an average grade, or a low grade? The literature recommends that assessments be authentic, that is, that they reflect real-world applications whenever possible. I'll show you what I do if you'd like."

"Yes, I'd appreciate that," said Mr. Edwards. "I'd also like to explore strategies for using peer evaluations and also portfolios, including electronic portfolios. I hear Mr. Boeck has a computer program for electronic portfolios."

"You have some challenging questions. Let's start with examples of how I design authentic performance assessments for my class. I'll bring some to our mentor-mentee meeting on Friday."

Questions for Reflection

1. What grades would you assign to Danielle in her various subjects? What is your rationale for assigning each grade?
2. What changes, if any, should Mr. Edwards make in his plan for assessing students? Why are those changes needed?

3. What are the advantages of identifying desired outcomes prior to designing activities and instructional goals?
4. How do you ensure congruence between outcomes, means of assessment, curriculum activities, and instructional goals?
5. To what extent would your system of grading and evaluation be based on achievement, on effort, on improvement, on other factors? Why do you emphisize certain factors over others?

Activities for Extending Thinking

1. Interview at least one experienced practicing teacher to determine (a) his or her desired student outcomes for a given unit and (b) the standards and criteria for assessing those outcomes.
2. Interview at least one experienced practicing teacher to determine how he or she uses assessment findings in planning for future teaching.
3. Outline a plan to assess the degree to which students use feedback on their written work. (Assumption: Rewrites will improve if students are graded on the degree to which they incorporate feedback into each new draft.)

Designing Your Own Case Planning and Preparation

Design a case related to planning and preparation for teaching. The story can focus on a method or strategy related to a single subject matter area (e.g., English or social studies) or on a more generic method or strategy pertinent to a wider range of subject matter areas. Some examples are

- Demonstrating knowledge of content and pedagogy
- Demonstrating knowledge of students
- Selecting instructional goals
- Demonstrating knowledge of resources
- Designing coherent instruction
- Assessing student learning*

In selecting a topic, reflect on recent or current field experiences, personal experiences as a student, or accounts of real classroom incidents. Include some demographic data that tell a bit about the community, school, classroom, teacher, students, and curriculum. Include at least one problem to which there is no obvious answer. Use fictitious names of persons and schools to maintain confidentiality.

Your case should be approximately two pages in length (typed, double-spaced) and should include three to four Questions for Reflection and one or two Activities for Extending Thinking. A form entitled "Designing Your Own Case" is provided on the following pages. It outlines categories for developing your case as well as for developing criteria for assessing responses to your Questions for Reflection and your Activities for Extending Thinking.

---

*The examples are from Danielson, C. (1996). *Enhancing professional practice: A framework for teaching.* Alexandria, VA: Association for Supervision and Curriculum Development.

Designing Your Own Case

Author Name(s): _____

Title of Case: _____ Grade Level(s): _____

Subject Matter Area (e.g., science)_____ (OR)

    Generic Teaching Topic (e.g., planning, grading): _____

Contextual Information: _____

    Community factors: _____

    School factors: _____

    Classroom factors: _____

        Teacher characteristics: _____

        Student characteristics: _____

        Characteristics of curriculum: _____

Story: _____

_____

_____

_____

_____

_____

Questions for Reflection:

1. _____

2. _____

3. _____

Activities for Extending Thinking:

1. _____

2. _____

Primary issue embedded in case (e.g., demonstrating knowledge of content, selecting instructional goals, assessing student learning):

_____

_____

Secondary issues(e.g., diversity in education, gender equity):_____

_____

_____

Criteria for assessing responses to your Questions for Reflection:

List criteria (e.g., response is clear, consistent with research or best practice, generalized to an appropriate degree—not overgeneralized, valid—based on facts in the case, relevant to an issue in the case, other):

1._____

2._____

3._____

Responses to Questions for Reflection:

List what you would consider to be examples of acceptable and unacceptable responses.

Acceptable	Unacceptable
1. a._____	_____
b._____	_____
2. a._____	_____
b._____	_____
3. a._____	_____
b._____	_____

Responses to Activities for Extended Thinking:

List examples of acceptable and unacceptable responses:

1. _____   _____

2. _____   _____

Suggested Readings

Brophy, J. E., & Good, T. L. (1986). Teacher behavior and student achievement. In M.C. Wittrock (Ed.), *Handbook of research on teaching* (3rd ed., pp. 328–375). New York: Macmillan.

Butler, R. (1987). Task-involving and ego-involving properties of evaluation. *Journal of Educational Psychology, 79*, 474–482.

Butler, R., & Nissan, M. (1986). Effects of no feedback, task-related comments, and grades on intrinsic motivation and performance. *Journal of Educational Psychology, 78*, 210–216.

Curriculum Development and Supplemental Materials Commission. (1991). *California basic instructional materials in English as a second language and foreign language* (adoption recommendations of the Curriculum Development and Supplemental Materials Commission to the State Board of Education, draft). Sacramento: California Department of Education.

Diez, M. E., & Moon, C. J. (1992). What do we want students to know?...and other important questions. *Educational Leadership, 49* (8), 38–41.

Druian, G., & Butler, J. (1987). *School Improvement Research Series. Research you can use.* Portland, OR: Northwest Regional Educational Laboratory. (ERIC Document Reproduction Service No. ED 291 145).

Emmer, E. T., Sanford, J. P., Clements, B.S., & Martin, J. (1982). *Improving classroom management and organization in junior high schools: An experiential investigation.* (R&D Report No. 6153). Austin: The University of Texas at Austin, Research and Development Center for Teacher Education.

Farr, R., & Tone, B. (1994). *Portfolio performance assessment.* Fort Worth: Harcourt Brace College Publishers.

Figueroa, R.A., & García, E. (1994). Issues in testing students from culturally and linguistically diverse backgrounds. *Multicultural Education, 2*(1), 10–19.

García, E., & Pearson, P. D. (1994). Assessment and diversity. In L. Darling-Hammond (Ed.), *Review of research in education* (Vol. 20, pp. 337–391). Washington, DC: American Educational Research Association.

Haberman, M. (1991). The pedagogy of poverty versus good teaching. *Phi Delta Kappan, 73*(4), 290–294.

Herman, J. L., & Winters, L. (1994). Portfolio research: A slim collection. *Educational Leadership, 52*(2), 48–55.

Hohn, R. (1986, October). *Research on contextual effects and effective teaching.* Paper presented at the Midwestern Educational Research Association Conference, Chicago. (ERIC Document Reproduction Service No. ED 287 853).

Irvine, J. J. (1990, May). Beyond role models: The influence of black teachers on black students. Paper presented at Educational Testing Service, Princeton, NJ.

Jones, J. (1992). *Praxis III Teacher Assessment Criteria Research Base.* Princeton, NJ: Educational Testing Service.

Kauchak, D., & Peterson, K. (1987). *Teachers' thoughts on the assessment of their teaching.* Washington, DC: American Educational Research Association.

Kohn, A. (1994). Grading: The issue is not how but why. *Educational Leadership, 52* (2), 38.

McCombs, B. L. (1992). *Learner-centered psychological principles: Guidelines for school redesign and reform.* Washington, DC: American Psychological Association.

National Board for Professional Teaching Standards. (1991). *Toward high and rigorous standards for the teaching profession* (3rd ed.). Detroit: Author.

Natriello, G. (1987). *Evaluation processes in schools and classrooms.* (Report No. 12). Baltimore: Center for Social Organization of Schools. (ERIC Document Reproduction Service No. ED 294 890).

Oakes, J. (1986). Tracking, inequity, and the rhetoric of school reform: Why schools don't change. *Journal of Education, 168* (1), 60-80.

Powell, R. R., Zehm, S., & García, J. (1996). *Field experience: Strategies for exploring diversity in schools.* Englewood Cliffs, NJ: Prentice Hall.

Reynolds, A. (1992). What is competent beginning teaching? A review of the literature. *Review of Educational Research 52* (1), 1-35.

Rosenshine, B. (1987). Explicit teaching and teacher training. *Journal of Teacher Education, 38*(3), 34-36.

Ruiz, R. (1991). The empowerment of language-minority students. In C. E. Sleeter (Ed.), *Empowerment through multicultural education* (pp. 217-227). Albany: State University of New York Press.

Shulman, L. S. (1987). Knowledge and teaching: Foundations of the new reform. *Harvard Educational Review, 57*(1), 1-22.

Stage, E. (1989). Strategies and materials for meeting the needs of all students in math, science, technology, and health. Sacramento: California Curriculum Commission.

Stiggins, R. J. (1994). *Student-centered classroom assessment.* New York: Macmillan College Publishing.

Sykes, G., & Bird, T. (1992). Teacher education and the case idea. *Review of Research in Education, 18,* 457-521.

Theobald, P., & Mills, E. (1995). Accountability and the struggle over what counts. *Phi Delta Kappan, 76* (6), 462-466.

Van Patten, J., Chao, C., & Reigeluth, C. (1986). A review of strategies for sequencing and synthesizing instruction. *Review of Educational Research 56* (4), 437-471.

Walker, H. (1985). Teacher social behavior standards and expectations as determinants of classroom ecology, teacher behavior, and child outcomes: Final report. Eugene: Center for Educational Policy and Management, University of Oregon.

Wiggins, G. (1993). Assessment: Authenticity, context, and validity. *Phi Delta Kappan, 75* (3), 200-214.

Part 3
The Classroom Environment

Creating Additional Context for a Given Case

Each case in this section is sufficiently complex to allow for multiple levels of analysis and multiple interpretations. Even so, it is important to bring your own knowledge and personal purpose to the analysis of a given case. Hence, the context within each case has purposely not been highly prescribed. For example, most of the cases purposely do not indicate the grade level, thereby allowing for a variety of readers to bring their own grade-level context to the case.

Therefore, as suggested in the introduction, prior to analyzing a given case, you are invited to modify its context. Your instructor will help decide which cases might be modified and the extent of the modifications and will direct you to do so individually, in small groups, or as a class.

When so directed by your instructor, include factors that make the case richer, more authentic, or more personally meaningful to you, your small group, or your class. You may want to re-create a context that resembles a school in which you are currently completing a field experience or in which you are teaching, or you may want to create a setting representing the type of school that you hope to work in some day. Include one or two factors from the following categories:

> *Characteristics of the community. You might include such factors as proportion of socioeconomic, ethnic, and religious groups and the sociopolitical attitudes of various community groups.*
>
> *Characteristics of the school. You might include demographics related to the ethnic, religious, and special needs make-up of the student body; curricular and extracurricular emphases of the school; and recent school reform efforts.*
>
> *Nature of the characters and the classroom. You might include information such as personal characteristics (e.g., physical appearance, social abilities, mannerisms and behavioral habits, intellectual abilities, and teaching or learning styles) or grade level of the class, physical arrangement of the classroom, type of curriculum, and daily schedule of the classes.*

For those cases identified by your instructor for analysis and for context modification, take a few minutes prior to analysis to list in writing several additional contextual variables that you believe are important.

Case 10

Students are given the opportunity to make real decisions regarding the operation of their classroom by helping to formulate rules for behavior.

Let's All Make Up the Rules

It was the first day of the new school year. After getting to know his students, Mr. Chu split the class into small groups. He explained to the students that since this was their classroom as well as his, they could help make the rules for conduct. He told each group to write out several rules to recommend to the class, as well as a consequence for breaking each rule. He monitored all the groups, making notes on each student's participation. After the groups completed the assignment, he collected their lists.

That evening he reviewed the lists and developed five rules that captured some aspects of each list. He stated the rules positively; for example, if a group had written "Never talk while someone else is talking," Mr. Chu wrote "Respect others," and he gave written examples, such as "listen when others are talking." He also included the consequence of breaking each rule, such as time-outs, loss of privileges, and detention.

When he had finished compiling the class list, he recalled observing that a number of the students had not participated in formulating rules and consequences for the class. He had not pressed them to contribute when he monitored the groups, but he was curious as to why they chose not to help create the rules. He noted further that two of the students were of Russian heritage, one a male, one a female and two were female students from Cambodia. Mr. Chu wondered whether cultural values, such as respect for and even dependence on adult authority, might have been the reason for their lack of response. He would ask them when he had a chance.

The next day, Mr. Chu explained how he had arrived at five collective class rules and consequences. After the class agreed that the list was acceptable, Mr. Chu wrote the rules in large letters on a sign and posted it at the front of the classroom. Mr. Chu felt confident that having ownership in the rules, students would be more likely to follow them.

Mr. Chu reminded the students that the next 10 minutes would be devoted to silent reading. He thought to himself, "Now would be the time to have a friendly chat with each of the four students who did not respond to my invitation to help make up the class rules." He knew he needed to be clear that he was not disappointed in them, but rather that he merely was interested in understanding why they did not participate in making up the rules.

Questions for Reflection

1. Was Mr. Chu rightfully concerned about the international students, or was he overreacting?
2. Should elementary students at any grade level be involved in developing classroom rules? If so, how would your approach vary for the different grade levels?
3. What are some other ways of stating rules negatively? How would you convert them to a positive format?
4. Develop a plan that you could implement in your classroom, including
   a. How you would involve students in developing the rules and procedures for classroom behavior
   b. The rules and procedures that you would hope to develop (with or without student involvement)
   c. The positive consequences of honoring the rules or procedures (if you would have positive consequences)
   d. The negative consequences of not honoring the rules or procedures (if you would have negative consequences)

Activity for Extending Thinking

1. Interview a school administrator, a school counselor, and a teacher to determine their views on involving students in establishing expectations for student behavior. Summarize your findings in writing and be prepared to share in class.

Case 11

A parent questions the display of photos of murals from the 1930s depicting stereotypical images of African Americans and women.

Overlook the Stereotypes—It's Art

It was parent conference night and Ms. Lotzer was saying goodnight to her last parent visitor when he said to her, "By the way, those large photos with the world maps on the bulletin board, did you know that they contain stereotypical images of Africans in loin-cloths and 'pickaninny hairstyles'? And one has 'Aunt Jemima-like' women picking cotton. They are really insulting!"

Ms. Lotzer responded: "You know, I never thought of that. Those are photos of murals that were donated to the school by the city—they're from a collection commissioned during the depression years to employ out-of-work artists. They were thought to have some artistic value. I believed they would be better for the children than blank walls, and they do accurately portray perceptions that existed in the 1930s."

"Well, that's true, but I don't think they send the right message! In fact, in addition to the ethnic stereotypes portrayed, three of them don't depict any female images at all!"

The next day Ms. Lotzer shared her experience with the principal. Sympathetic to the parent's concern, the principal ordered the photos covered until it was decided whether they should be permanently removed.

The following day in class, Ms. Lotzer's students asked, "Why are the photos covered?" She told them of the events of the previous day, being careful to maintain the anonymity of the parent involved. She also mentioned that the photos would remain covered until the next faculty meeting. "At that time, I will present the parent's concerns and I hope we can agree on a reasonable policy; but for now the photos will be covered," she said.

Some of her students seemed to support the decision of the principal, while others did not agree with his decision to cover the photos. The students asked Ms. Lotzer, "What do you plan to do?"

"I'm not sure what I'll say," she replied. "It would be helpful, though, to know what you think—both as individuals and as a class.

It would also be helpful to know what more parents think," she said. "Perhaps we could devise several survey questions for your parents and compile the responses. Then, I can represent not only my own views, but also those of you and your parents. Are you willing to do that?" she asked.

Hearing no objection, Ms. Lotzer asked: "Who can think of a first question that we could include in our survey?"

Questions for Reflection

1. Do you agree or disagree with the principal's decision to cover the photos?
2. What principles should teachers follow in
   a. Selecting materials for display
   b. Involving students and parents in decisions regarding such issues
3. How appropriate is it for a teacher to survey parents without prior approval of the principal? Explain.
4. How can displayed materials contribute to a positive culture of learning, that is, a culture in which the teachers and students care about the content to be learned and the process through which it is learned?
5. How can displayed materials encourage high expectations for learning?

Activity for Extending Thinking

1. Examine the classroom bulletin boards and display areas of several classrooms to determine whether their content contributes to the establishment of a culture for learning. In what ways, if any, do displayed materials encourage high expectations for learning?

Case 12

A student publicly objects to the inclusion of a classmate in his small group because, as he claims, the classmate is "gay."

Not in My Group—He's Gay

Ms. Collins was a firm believer in education that was multicultural and had the potential to lead to social reform. She organized her curriculum around issues of race, gender, class, disability, language, and affectional orientation. She used the lives of students in her classes as the starting point for addressing such issues.

On this day Ms. Collins's students were busily engaged in heterogeneous small group discussions about their family heritage projects. She had asked them to share the information about their ethnic heritage that they had obtained from their parents or guardians the night before. Ms. Collins hoped that not only would the small group discussions give her pupils opportunities to express themselves, but they might also help identify differences and similarities among classmates. Certainly, she thought, it would help them be more thoughtful about what else they would need to find out in order to make their projects more complete.

As she moved to the small group of students in the rear of the room, Xeng, a Hmong student new to the class, said to her as he pointed to a classmate named Kim: "Keep him away from me—he's gay!" The other group members covered their mouths and laughed.

Ms. Collins was caught by surprise. Consistent enforcement of class rules established at the beginning of the school year had prevented the use of such labels in her class until today. She noticed that Kim appeared embarrassed by Xeng's accusation.

"Do you know what 'gay' means?" she asked, convinced Xeng was just repeating something he had heard an adult say that without knowing what it meant.

"Yes," replied Xeng. "It's when one man has sex with another man."

Ms. Collins was baffled. She thought to herself, "Should I ask Xeng if he is sure, or how he knows that Kim is gay? Should I ask Xeng if he is angry with Kim, and, if so, why? Should I reprimand Xeng for making his judgment public? How should I respond to Kim?"

Questions for Reflection

1. What is the central issue in this situation?

2. List possible factors that may have motivated Xeng to say what he said about Kim. What personal needs might Xeng have been trying to satisfy?
3. How would you model *caring for* students and promote *caring of* students for one another in this situation?
4. Under what conditions, if any, would you involve the class in a discussion of this issue? Write down the actual opening statements/questions you would use to introduce such a discussion.
5. What other incidents regarding affectional preference have you observed in schools? How were they addressed? How should they have been addressed?

Activities for Extending Thinking

1. Discuss with an experienced practicing teacher the strategies he or she uses to create and maintain a classroom environment of respect and rapport with students. List those strategies in writing and be prepared to share in class.
2. Discuss with an advocate of a traditionally underrepresented group recommendations for developing a *safe* environment for all students.

Case 13

Several students play a joke on a female classmate by telling a learning disabled pupil that she has a crush on him.

We Only Meant It As a Joke

Mr. Carr consistently modeled respect for all students. He made sure that mainstreamed students were socialized into his class by providing an opportunity for them to work in heterogeneous, cooperative groups; share leadership roles; and generally contribute equally to classroom life. He was careful to praise and encourage all students equally.

One of the classroom procedures posted on the front wall was "Respect others." Students understood what this meant—they had been given numerous specific examples on the first day of class.

For the first six weeks of the term, Mr. Carr's students honored the procedures listed. Then one day, several of them were moved to have what they considered fun with Mia, one of their classmates. They suggested to Mike, a learning disabled student, that Mia had expressed an interest in him and that he should call her and ask her to be his girlfriend. They intended that the "joke" would be on Mia.

That evening Mike called Mia. Mia politely replied that she did not want a boy friend.

When Mr. Carr heard of the scheme, he immediately thought about how he would enforce the classroom rule that students respect others. Of course, the students would have to pay the consequences established on the first day of school. Mr. Carr believed in being consistent in maintaining standards for behavioral conduct. Now he was faced with the question of how to best make this situation a learning experience.

Questions for Reflection

1. What consequence(s) would be appropriate for the students causing the problem for Mike and Mia?
2. What might you say to Mike that would be helpful to him? (Write out your response.)
3. What would you say to Mia? (Write out your response.)
4. What could Mr. Carr do to help all his students be more respectful of those with special needs?

5. What would you recommend that Mr. Carr do if the parents of the perpetrators were prominent, wealthy and influential community members who refused to have consequences imposed on their children?

Activity for Extending Thinking

1. Discuss with at least one special education teacher the most prevalent types of interaction problems that occur between students with special needs and (a) teachers and (b) regular education students, and what he or she would do to prevent such problems.

Case 14

A teacher tries to establish clear standards for behavior as well as develop in students a disposition for respecting others.

Respect? Let's Talk About It

It was the second week of school. Ms. Martin was frustrated with her students. Despite her efforts at establishing and posting clear rules and consequences for behavior, several of her students were still disrespectful to others.

On Monday of the third week, Ms. Martin asked the class, "What does 'respect' mean?" Patrick raised his hand and answered, "I think respect means being kind and helpful." Ms. Martin replied, "What is an example of what you mean?" Patrick then told a story of how he had helped one of his friends with an art project. Ms. Martin thanked him for his good example.

Other students raised their hands and offered examples of respecting others' feelings and beliefs. Lee, a Vietnamese student, noted that in his culture it is respectful to look down rather than into the eyes of an adult during a conversation. Mohammed, a Muslim student from Somalia, agreed. Barry acknowledged that in his Native American tradition, when walking past someone it is a sign of respect to walk in front of the person rather than behind as in white culture. He explained further that passing in front of the person allows him or her to see that you intend no harm. James, an African American, said that confronting him clearly and directly with instructions was a sign of respect in his family. Liz, a Native American student, noted that an example from her tribal culture would be to take 10 days to honor the death of an uncle or cousin or other family member. The class discussed these and other examples offered by the students. Examples of what it was like *not* to be respectful were also given.

Ms. Martin listened and acknowledged each student's contribution. She then shared some stories of her own friends, including times when her feelings were hurt because someone had mistreated her. Finally, she related the class discussion to established class rules and reminded students to encourage others in following the procedures.

After the discussion, Ms. Martin asked her students if they would like to decorate a bulletin board using respect as the theme. They seemed to like the idea.

Questions for Reflection

1. Assess Ms. Martin's discussion of respect as a way to establish standards of conduct?
2. What would you have done to make Ms. Martin's discussion even more effective?
3. What topics other than "kindness" and "respect" might you use in discussing behavior management issues with students?
4. What strategies can a teacher use to teach students to encourage each other to help monitor classroom procedures and routines?

Activities for Extending Thinking

1. Interview three teachers about the strategies they use to establish clear expectations for behavior?
2. Videotape a teaching episode by a teacher, an education student in a field experience, or yourself. Analyze the tape to identify ways that teachers and students monitor student behavior.

Case 15

Aware that a student in her class is from a home devoid of support, a teacher encourages all students to show compassion.

Let's Be Nice to Ricardo

Ms. Anderson was having trouble with two students in her class. Tommy and Ricardo were often rude to their fellow students and did not seem to care about their classmates' feelings. They used profanity and physical threats. No matter how many times a day Ms. Anderson reminded and reprimanded Tommy and Ricardo, they did not seem to change.

One day Ms. Anderson offered them a deal. For every time they were thoughtful of another student—when they offered to help, when they shared, when they said positive things about classmates—they would receive a point. When they each reached 20 points, they would be allowed to choose a reward from a predetermined list that they and Ms. Anderson devised. The point total would be displayed on a chart at Ms. Anderson's desk for Ricardo and Tommy to see whenever they wished.

Because Ricardo was from a troubled home, Ms. Anderson tried to be a bit more forgiving of his failures to follow the class rules. She knew that his misbehavior was a result of emotional abuse at home. She often made private comments to individual students, such as "Let's be nice to Ricardo—he has a tough life." She tried to make his life a bit better by not demanding quite as much in achievement or conduct.

Tommy enjoyed the challenge and began to say "please" and "thank you" to fellow students and always asked permission before using their belongings. He stopped making rude comments to the other students and even played with them without incident. Ms. Anderson told Tommy she was pleased with the change in his behavior.

Ricardo's improvement was not as dramatic. He seemed to be trying most of the time, yet some evidence of anger and frustration became apparent at other times. Ms. Anderson was not quite sure what to make of his inconsistent behavior.

Questions for Reflection

1. What are the strengths of the approach Ms. Anderson took in monitoring the behavior of Tommy and Ricardo?

2. What are the weaknesses of her approach?
3. What other approaches might Ms. Anderson have used to help Ricardo and Tommy? On what theory(ies) is (are) your recommendations based?
4. How might the family and cultural background of the students play a role in this case?
5. Is expectation theory an issue in this story? If so, explain.

Activity for Extending Thinking

1. Review at least three current research studies on the effects of teacher expectations on student achievement. Summarize your findings for the class.

Case 16

A classroom Christmas tree and other winter holiday symbols cause students to question the teacher's intent.

Isn't the Christmas Tree a Christian Symbol?

It was the first week of December. The previous day Ms. Halverson had added to her bulletin boards some holiday wishes, including "Merry Christmas," "Happy Hanukkah," and "Happy Kwanza." In addition, she had placed a small two-foot-tall Christmas tree in the front corner of the room by her desk.

Several of her students had entered the room a few minutes before class was to begin. The students were of Russian, Chinese, and Egyptian heritage. They made a few comments to one another and then addressed Ms Halverson: "Ms. Halverson, you told us to let you know if we felt that our classroom was not as inclusive as it could possibly be. . . . Well, isn't the Christmas tree a symbol of the Christian religion?" asked Yen. "And by having a Christmas tree, aren't you emphasizing one religion over another?"

Ms. Halverson nodded as Yen spoke: "Well, yes, you're right. Actually it's a pre-Christian symbol that arose in Europe. But I meant to simply acknowledge it as one of the most prevalent historical and cultural symbols in the United States," she replied.

Yen responded: "So you didn't mean it to be taken as a preferred religious symbol?"

"No, not at all—merely as a historical and cultural artifact," replied Ms. Halverson. "I'm glad that you raised the issue. I now realize that I need to clarify for the class just what my intentions are regarding the tree. Thanks for being sensitive to those who might have other interpretations. It's exactly this kind of feedback that I need in order to make our class more inclusive! Perhaps you and the class can offer some suggestions for making our room look more inclusive during the holidays." The students seemed eager to help.

Questions for Reflection

1. Should Ms. Halverson have placed a Christmas tree in her room? Why or why not?

2. How adequate was Ms. Halverson's explanation and justification to the students?
3. What factors in the cultrual context of a classroom, school, and community might appropriately affect a teacher's decision to display or not display an object that does or could have some religious meaning?
4. Comment on the interaction between the teacher and Yen. What did Ms. Halverson say or do that would tend to demonstrate respect and caring for Yen?
5. In general, what can teachers say and do to develop an environment of respect and rapport in the classroom?

Activities for Extending Thinking

1. Discuss with a school administrator the school policies regarding the use or display of objects that have or could have some religious meaning.
2. Discuss with a practicing teacher the methods he or she uses to demonstrate affection, caring, and respect for students.

Case 17

Students perform assigned tasks in a class activity and receive encouragement and praise from their teacher for their efforts.

Your Data Are So Neatly Recorded

It was the last week of school before the spring break. For the past two weeks, Ms. Bell's class had worked hard on a series of lab experiments focused on factors affecting the growth rate of seeds and young pea plants. The students had demonstrated pride in learning about the structure and function of seeds and in getting their seeds to grow.

On this particular Monday, as students were completing the final lab in the series, Ms. Bell circulated throughout the room, privately acknowledging the contributions of various groups of students. "I want to tell you how proud I am of your work," she said to the members of one group. "Randolf and Jon, you did especially well in creating hypotheses prior to testing the effects of temperature and light. Your ideas took into account our prior learning and at the same time were creative. Mia and Amy, your work in recording the data for your group is commendable. Your records are easier to read because they are so neatly done."

To the second group, Ms. Bell said, "Rod and Chang, your predictions as to what would happen in all of the labs in this unit were right on target! You have a good grasp of the principles of plant growth. And Sonya and Angie, your help in organizing the materials for the experiments and in checking the measurements of the plants was great. Your group couldn't have gotten the correct results without you!"

Ms. Bell provided similar feedback to the remaining two groups. All of the students seemed appreciative of her comments.

About five minutes before the bell was to ring, Ms. Bell reminded the students of their responsibilities for cleanup and storage of lab materials. "Be sure you water your plants and return them to the window," she said. The students seemed to know their responsibilities and they moved carefully to store their plants and clean their tables.

Questions for Reflection

1. What was effective and ineffective about Ms. Bell's interaction with students in this case?
2. Assume that the reinforcement pattern evident in these exchanges is typical of the feedback given by Ms. Bell during the term. What effect would you suspect Ms. Bell's interaction would have on
   a. Her students' achievements
   b. Their feelings of respect for their work
   c. Their self-expectations for learning in science
   d. The culture for learning in the classroom
3. What principles should a teacher follow in order to promote positive habits of the mind (e.g., critical thinking and learning and self-regulated thinking and learning)? List some specific strategies you could implement in your classroom to address such goals.
4. What, if any, issues of diversity are embedded in this case?

Activity for Extending Thinking

1. Teach a lesson in an accessible school—if you are currently in a field experience or are teaching, you may want to arrange to teach your lesson in that school. Videotape the lesson and analyze the tape for patterns of teacher-student interaction. Are there individuals and/or groups of students with whom you have more or less interaction? What types of interactions do you have with various individuals and groups (e.g., interactions that stimulate higher levels of thinking)? How do students interact with one another? List the interaction patterns you have identified. Be prepared to share in class.

Case 18

Moving from a large group to a small group activity presents a problem for a primary teacher.

No, This Is My Chair!

It was the third week of school and Ms. Herrera was proud of the positive classroom climate that she had been able to establish in her second grade room. Students were polite and well mannered and usually followed the clearly defined classroom procedures that Ms. Herrera and they had collaboratively established. There was but one problem, a problem that arose when students moved from the large group activity to a small group project activity.

Ms. Herrera had discussed the procedures for transition from large to small groups. Students knew they were to (1) walk in an orderly manner to their designated table, (2) select a chair, and (3) without talking, sit down in it. The first few times they made the transition, students followed the procedures. On the next occasions, however, students at some of the tables seemed to be attracted to the same chair.

At one table for example, as Carlos placed his hand on the back of a chair to pull it out, Melissa grabbed the seat of the same chair. "This is my seat!" she exclaimed. Only a moment later Alex countered, "No, this is my chair!" The only thing stopping Amy, the final group member, from grabbing the same chair was the fact that Ms. Herrera got there first.

"Please," she said, "Let's not argue over the same chair. There are enough for everyone." She pointed to each chair and called out the name of one of the students. Each grudgingly took his or her assigned seat. "That's not fair," said Carlos, "I got there first!" Amy and Melissa both gave Ms. Herrera a surly look as if to agree that she had not been fair.

At two other tables a similar scene took place. Ms. Herrera knew that her positive classroom atmosphere had suffered. After school Ms. Herrera shared her new challenge with Mr. Ramos.

"Want to know what I do?" Mr. Ramos asked.

"Yes, please," she responded.

"I take a 4 × 6 card, punch two holes and attach a string," he said, demonstrating as he spoke. "Then I write each student's first name on one of the cards. Just before the students move to the tables, I drape each name tag over a chair. Students then go to the chair with their name on it. I've had no problems with the system."

    "I'll try it," said Ms. Herrera. "Thanks!"

Questions for Reflection

1. Write a brief general assessment of Ms. Herrera's initial problem in moving from one activity to another.
2. What specific steps, other than the name tag plan, could she take to ensure that such transitions between activities go more smoothly?
3. What are some other common problems of managing classroom procedures, for example, distributing materials and supplies or performing noninstructional duties such as taking attendance? Identify a promising solution for each problem listed.

Activity for Extending Thinking

1. Discuss with at least one practicing teacher specific practical strategies for ensuring smooth transitions among activities. Be prepared to summarize your insights in class.

Designing Your Own Case
Classroom Environment

Design a case related to classroom environment. The story can focus on a method or strategy related to a single subject matter area (e.g., English or social studies) or on a more generic method or strategy pertinent to a wider range of subject matter areas. Some examples are

- Creating an environment of respect and rapport
- Establishing a culture for learning
- Managing classroom procedures
- Managing student behavior
- Organizing physical space*

In selecting a topic, reflect on recent or current field experiences, personal experiences as a student, or accounts of real classroom incidents. Include some demographic data that tell a bit about the community, school, classroom, teacher, students, and curriculum. Include at least one problem to which there is no obvious answer. Use fictitious names of persons and schools to maintain confidentiality.

Your case should be approximately two pages in length (typed, double-spaced) and should include three to four Questions for Reflection and one or two Activities for Extending Thinking. A form entitled "Designing Your Own Case" is provided on the following pages. It outlines categories for developing your case as well as for developing criteria for assessing responses to your Questions for Reflection and your Activities for Extending Thinking.

---

*The examples are from Danielson, C. (1996). *Enhancing professional practice: A framework for teaching.* Alexandria, VA: Association for Supervision and Curriculum Development.

Designing Your Own Case

Author Name(s): _____

Title of Case: _____ Grade Level(s): _____

Subject Matter Area (e.g., science):_____ (OR)

    Generic Teaching Topic (e.g., teacher interaction with students, managing student behavior): _____

Contextual Information: _____

    Community factors:_____

    School factors: _____

    Classroom factors: _____

        Teacher characteristics: _____

        Student characteristics: _____

        Characteristics of curriculum: _____

Story: _____._____

_____

_____

_____

_____

Questions for Reflection:

1._____

2._____

3._____

Activities for Extending Thinking:

1._____

2._____

Primary issue embedded in case (e.g., establishing a culture for learning, managing student behavior):

_____

_____

Secondary issues (e.g., diversity in education, gender equity):_____

_____

_____

Criteria for assessing responses to your Questions for Reflection:

List criteria (e.g., response is clear, consistent with research or best practice, generalized to an appropriate degree—not overgeneralized, valid—based on facts in the case, relevant to an issue in the case, other):

1._____

2._____

3._____

Responses to Questions for Reflection:

List what you would consider to be examples of acceptable and unacceptable responses.

Acceptable	Unacceptable
1. a._____	_____
b._____	_____
2. a._____	_____
b._____	_____
3. a._____	_____
b._____	_____

Responses to Activities for Extended Thinking:

List examples of acceptable and unacceptable responses:

1. _____	_____
2. _____	_____

Suggested Readings

Anderson, L. W. (1986). Research on teaching and educational effectiveness. *National Association of Secondary School Principals Curriculum Report, 15,* 4 (entire issue). (ERIC Document Reproduction Service No. ED 269 868).

Brophy, J. E. (1987). Educating teachers about managing classrooms and students. Occasional Paper No. 115. East Lansing: Institute for Research on Teaching, Michigan State University.

Brophy, J. E., & Good, T. L. (1986). Teacher behavior and student achievement. In M. C. Wittrock (Eds.). *Handbook of research on teaching* (3rd ed., pp. 328–375). New York: Macmillan.

Emans, R., & Milburn, C. (1989). *The knowledge base of teaching: A review and commentary of process-product research.* Vermillion: The University of South Dakota School of Education.

Emmer, E. T., Everston, C. M., Sanford, J. P., Clements, B. S., & Worsham, M. E. (1989). *Classroom management for secondary teachers* (2nd ed.). Englewood Cliffs, NJ: Prentice Hall.

Everston, C. M. (1989). Improving classroom management: A school-based program for beginning the year. *Journal of Educational Research, 83* (2), 82–90.

Everston, C. M., & Harris, A. H. (1992). What we know about managing classrooms. *Educational Leadership, 49* (7), 74–78.

Fraser, B. J. (1986). *Classroom environment.* London: Groom Helm.

Goss, S. S., & Ingersoll, G. M. (1981). *Management of disruptive and off-task behaviors: Selected resources.* Washington, DC: ERIC Clearinghouse on Teacher Education. (ERIC Document Reproduction No. SP 017 373).

Irvine, J. J. (1990). *Beyond role models: The influence of black teachers on black students.* Paper presented at Educational Testing Service, Princeton, NJ.

Leinhardt, G. (1992). What research on learning tells us about teaching. *Educational Leadership, 49* (7), 20–25.

Morine-Dershimer, G. (1977). *What's in a plan? Stated and unstated plans for lessons.* Sacramento: California State Commission for Teacher Preparation and Licensing. (ERIC Document Reproduction No. ED 139 739).

U.S. Department of Education. (1987). *What works: Research about teaching and learning.* Washington, DC: U.S. Government Printing Office.

Walberg, H., Schiller, D., & Haertel, G. D. (1979). The great revolution in educational research. *Phi Delta Kappan, 61* (3), 179–182.

Ysseldyke, J., Christenson, S., & Thurlow, M. L. (1987). *Instructional factors that influence student achievement: An integrative review.* (Monograph No. 7). Minneapolis: University of Minnesota Instructional Alternatives Project.

Part 4
Instruction

Creating Additional Context for a Given Case

Each case in this section is sufficiently complex to allow for multiple levels of analysis and multiple interpretations. Even so, it is important to bring your own knowledge and personal purpose to the analysis of a given case. Hence, the context within each case has purposely not been highly prescribed. For example, most of the cases purposely do not indicate the grade level, thereby allowing for a variety of readers to bring their own grade-level context to the case.

Therefore, as suggested in the introduction, prior to analyzing a given case, you are invited to modify its context. Your instructor will help decide which cases might be modified and the extent of the modifications and will direct you to do so individually, in small groups, or as a class.

When so directed by your instructor, include factors that make the case richer, more authentic, or more personally meaningful to you, your small group, or your class. You may want to re-create a context that resembles a school in which you are currently completing a field experience or in which you are teaching, or you may want to create a setting representing the type of school that you hope to work in some day. Include one or two factors from the following categories:

> *Characteristics of the community. You might include such factors as proportion of socioeconomic, ethnic, and religious groups and the sociopolitical attitudes of various community groups.*
>
> *Characteristics of the school. You might include demographics related to the ethnic, religious, and special needs make-up of the student body; curricular and extracurricular emphases of the school; and recent school reform efforts.*
>
> *Nature of the characters and the classroom. You might include information such as personal characteristics (e.g., physical appearance, social abilities, mannerisms and behavioral habits, intellectual abilities, and teaching or learning styles) or grade level of the class, physical arrangement of the classroom, type of curriculum, and daily schedule of the classes.*

For those cases identified by your instructor for analysis and for context modification, take a few minutes prior to analysis to list in writing several additional contextual variables that you believe are important.

Case 19

Two students ask permission to focus their project on Native American heroes rather than the Mount Rushmore presidents assigned by the teacher.

Can We Study Crazy Horse?

Ms. Williams was in her third year of teaching. She often referred to her work as "a privilege rather than a job."

This year, as in the past, Ms. Williams decided to include learning activities that were based on current events. From a newspaper article telling of the U.S. government's intent to clean and restore the Mount Rushmore monument (at a cost of $56 million), she designed a small group project. Students would be required to summarize the major accomplishments of a president honored at Mount Rushmore, as well as identify his admirable traits. Ms. Williams thought that the project requirement would teach some important historical concepts, refine the students' research skills, and also give them another opportunity to learn cooperatively.

On the day that she introduced the project to the class, she gave each student a list of the presidents honored on Mount Rushmore—Washington, Jefferson, Lincoln, and Theodore Roosevelt. She also gave them an outline of the material to be included in the final report.

After class, two students, Mary Bearrunner and Beth Whiteman, asked Ms. Williams if they could do their project on an American Indian chief such as Crazy Horse, rather than one of the presidents. With great conviction, they said that even though the presidents on Mount Rushmore had done some good for whites, each had a hand in what some would call racist acts against Native Americans. "For example," said Beth, "Jefferson bought land from France that actually belonged to Native American people. And Lincoln approved the mass execution of 38 Indians in Mankato, Minnesota."

Ms. Williams said she would need to think about it and would let them know the next day.

Questions for Reflection

1. Write out the response you would give to Mary and Beth if you were their teacher.
2. To what extent might the cultural make-up of the class affect your response?

3. What principles of inclusiveness should guide a teacher's decision to adjust assignments such as the one in this case?
4. To what extent might you adjust your lesson and explore with your class the alleged "racist acts" of the presidents? Explain your response.

Activity for Extending Thinking

1. Think of a topic (e.g., dinosaurs, spiders, animals) that you might teach to students either in your current clinical setting or a future job. Design an inventory to assess students' needs and interests related to the topic. Include items such as, "If you could study any animal, which would you choose?" Administer the inventory to elementary students. How flexible and responsive could you be in meeting all the needs and interests of the students surveyed?

Case 20

Two Latina students ask their teacher to study a folk hero other than one on her list of traditional North American folk heroes.

Folk Heroes—
Is Cesar Chavez One?

As in previous years, Ms. Rohlfs required her students to complete a small group project in which they were to summarize the major accomplishments of a "North American folk hero." Her goals were for students to refine their research and writing skills, to learn how to do collaborative work, and to learn positive values and character lessons that she believed were needed in a society of increasing crime and violence.

On the day that she introduced the project to the class, she gave each student a list of folk heroes from which they could choose. The list included Paul Bunyan, John Henry, Davy Crockett, and Johnny Appleseed.

After class, two students, Rita Martinez and Beth Ruiz, asked Ms. Rohlfs if they could do their project on Cesar Chavez, Calamity Jane, Harriet Tubman, Sacajawea, or another famous frontiersperson or leader in American history. They argued that such heroes also teach healthy values and that they would be more interested in their research if they could choose their topic. Ms. Rohlfs said she would need to think about it and would let them know the next day.

Questions for Reflection

1. Write out the response you would give to Rita and Beth.
2. List the strengths and weaknesses of Ms. Rohlfs's lesson on American folk heroes.
3. List the aspects of the lesson that you would modify. Why would you make those adjustments (that is, what situations would call for such modification)?
4. Describe any similar experiences you have observed in schools in which students have asked for adjustments in assignments.

Activity for Extending Thinking

1. Discuss with colleagues the issue of making adjustments in topics or problems they might study. Explore issues related to what is a reasonable number (range) of choices. How limited should "limited choice" be? Give concrete examples.

Case 21

Thanksgiving celebrations of five different cultures are compared in a small group reading activity.

Other Cultures Celebrate Thanksgiving Too

It was mid-November when Mr. Rodriguez began his lesson on "Giving Thanks in Different Lands." He read the lesson objectives from the blackboard to his class:"Today we will learn how people of the United States have celebrated 'Thanksgiving,' as well as how people of other countries give thanks."

"How many of you have celebrated Thanksgiving?" he asked. Nearly all of the students raised a hand. "Please take out a sheet of paper and write what you know about Thanksgiving celebrations. Your papers will not be graded. I just want to know what you already know about our topic."

After several minutes, it appeared that all had finished writing. Mr. Rodriguez collected the papers and then read a brief story entitled "The First Thanksgiving," a traditional account of how the English settlers gave thanks for their good fortune. Mr. Rodriguez raised a number of questions about the historical accuracy of the account, including whether Native Americans would have likely helped in the celebration.

"Class, now that you have heard the usual story about the 'First Thanksgiving,' I would like to extend our thinking about celebrations of thanks. It turns out that Native Americans actually had celebrations of thanks before the English arrived in this land." For the next two minutes, Mr. Rodriguez read a short story about the "First Fruits Ceremony" and the "Green Corn Ceremony" of the Wampanoags of Plymouth, Massachusetts, noting the cultural significance of each celebration.

"Now," he said, "I have stories of how four other cultures gave thanks for what they considered to be important. I have assigned pairs. I will give each pair two stories of thanksgiving celebrations of people of other lands. I would like each of you to read one story to your partner. Take your time in reading. Your goal is to understand both of the stories completely. We will discuss them when everyone is done."

Mr. Rodriguez passed out the stories. They were

"First Fruits" celebration of the African Zulu

"Mid-Autumn Festival" of many Chinese people in San Francisco's Chinatown

"Dia de Gracias" of native people of Mexico (including the Olmecas, Zapotecas, Mayas, Toltecas, Mixtecas, and Haustecas)

"Sukkot" or "Feast of the Tabernacles" celebrated by Jewish people

When the students were finished reading to one another, Mr. Rodriguez asked them to share the key aspects of each celebration with the class. He recorded critical elements of each story in four columns on the board.

He then asked, "What are some similarities about how all four groups give thanks?" After listing several, he asked, "What are some differences?" Finally, as the period was drawing to a close, he asked, "What general principles have we learned about different groups of people and how they give thanks for what they have?" Again he listed student responses on the board.

"What have we learned about broadening our perspectives or extending our understanding of the meaning of 'First' in 'First Thanksgiving'?"

"Tomorrow," he concluded, "we will talk more about how you give thanks as well as what today's lesson might mean to you personally. Good job today! See you tomorrow."

Questions for Reflection

1. What did Mr. Rodriguez do to help students *acquire* knowledge about Thanksgiving celebrations? What is your assessment of his technique?
2. What did Mr. Rodriguez do to *extend and refine* their knowledge about Thanksgiving celebrations? List the lesson steps that he had students follow.
3. How would Mr. Rodriguez's method for presenting information help students learn how to think? Would you imagine that his methods would engage students in learning in classrooms generally? Why or why not?
4. How can a lesson such as this one contribute to goals of multiculturalism? Describe other kinds of lessons that can contribute to goals of multiculturalism.

Activity for Extending Thinking

1. Discuss with practicing teachers methods they use for intellectually engaging students with content, or as some would say, methods for getting students to "actively construct meaning." For

example, in teaching a skill, a teacher might tell about the skill, model (demonstrate) it, have students practice the skill with guidance, and then have students practice the skill independently. Such a sequence is both logical and supported by research. In teaching a concept, the teacher might define the concept, give examples and nonexamples of it, have students give examples and nonexamples, and have students demonstrate how to apply the concept. List specific and/or general methods of engagement suggested by teachers interviewed.

Case 22

*A student teacher and her cooperating teacher each
use a different approach with a pupil who has lost an
assignment stored on the computer.*

Let's Start with What You Have Done

Mary, a quiet student of Ojibwe heritage, had already written two of the three poems required by her teacher, Mr. Arnold, for the poetry assignment. For her third poem, Mary chose to write a special poem about her mother, describing just how much she cared for her. Mary planned to frame it and give it to her mother on her birthday.

At the end of the class period, the day before it was due and the day before her mother's birthday, Mary realized that the computer disk on which the poem had been stored was not in the book in which she had put it. She checked her other books, then her backpack. It was nowhere.

Mary was horrified. Not only would she get an incomplete, but even worse, she would not have the poem ready for her mother's birthday.

Mr. Arnold noticed a tear in Mary's eye. With the other students working on their computers, Mr. Arnold approached Mary.

"What's the trouble, Mary?" he asked caringly.

Sobbing softly, Mary explained.

"That's too bad," replied Mr. Arnold. "If only you had saved it to the hard drive too. I saw you nod when I asked if you understood how to save material; I thought you knew. Well, don't let it worry you. I'll give you an extra day, perhaps you can come up with a shorter poem that will at least get you partial credit."

Noticing Duncan waving his hand for help, Mr. Arnold left Mary's desk. Ms. Denesen, Mr. Arnold's student teacher from the local college, stepped in.

"Mary, I heard what happened. I'm sure your loss does matter to you. It's difficult when you lose something you've worked hard on and that you like." Ms. Denesen paused and then continued, "Do you have any of the ideas written down anywhere else?"

Mary replied, "Yes, I did write a few of my thoughts in my notebook when I was just starting."

"Good," said Ms. Denesen. "Let's start with what you have and go from there. And this time we'll save it on the hard drive and a disk and make a hard copy too. I can help you at noon today and tomorrow in class if you'd like, OK?"

Mary seemed to feel better.

Questions for Reflection

1. Compare the responses of Mr. Arnold and Ms. Denesen to Mary's loss. What message does each response send? How would each affect Mary? How would each affect the classroom climate?
2. What specific skills did Ms. Denesen employ when responding to Mary? What are the important elements of good feedback? How important is it to listen to and acknowledge thoughts and feelings of students before providing feedback?
3. Could some students view Ms. Denesen's approach as patronizing? If so, how would you modify it?
4. Did Ms. Denesen overstep her authority? Should she have asked Mr. Arnold about helping Mary before stepping in?
5. What principles would guide you in deciding how to respond to a student with a problem like Mary's; for example, can using models of exemplary work be helpful?

Activity for Extending Thinking

1. Scholars have said that feedback should be immediate, ongoing, accurate, substantive, specific, and constructive. Define each of these and give an example of how you might integrate each into a typical feedback episode with a student.

Case 23

A teacher considers varying opinions from colleagues regarding acceptance of student use of Black English Vernacular.

You'll Need Both Black Vernacular and Standard English

Mr. Drake had corrected the creative writing homework assignment from the previous day. He had wrestled with one particular paper written by Matt Williams, an African American student who was new to the school. Mr. Drake was unsure how to handle Matt's use of Black English Vernacular (BEV). Throughout the paper were statements in which "be" was used as a finite verb, statements such as "He be happy and nice," and "When they both be home, they usually be working around the house." And there were other differences in the use of grammar, differences such as using "done" to note that an action had been completed, as in "She done finished it"; the use of double or triple negatives, as in "They ain't got no car"; and the use of "f" for "th" as in "wif" for "with".

At lunch Mr. Drake approached Ms. Grover, a trusted colleague in the classroom next to him. He showed her Matt's paper. Ms. Grover read several paragraphs. "If I were you, I'd tell him that if I accepted this form of language, he would never learn to operate in society—that he would be at a disadvantage when applying for jobs. Moreover, I'd tell him that Black English Vernacular is a deviation from correct, Standard English." Mr. Drake thanked her for her advice.

Mr. Drake also shared his problem with Ms. Manning. He knew she was taking a continuing education course on sociolinguistics at a nearby college. She was interested in his dilemma.

"Would you like to hear a few lines about dialects from our course text?" she asked.

Mr. Drake nodded.

Ms. Manning read:

> The fact is, however, that standard English is only one variety among many, although a peculiarly important one. Linguistically speaking, it cannot even legitimately be considered better than other varieties. The scientific study of all language has convinced scholars that all languages, and correspondingly all dialects, are equally "good" as linguistic systems. All varieties of a language are structured, complex, rule-governed systems that are wholly adequate for their speakers.... There is nothing at all inherent in non-

standard varieties that makes them inferior. Any apparent inferiority is due only to their association with speakers from underprivileged, low-status groups.*

When she had finished, she told Mr. Drake of three students in her classes, each of whom used a different form of Black English. She explained to him that Amy, from New York, might say, for example, "Let's get ready to roll to the store"; while Darnelle, from Georgia, might say, "Let's be fiddin [fixing] to go to tha sto"; and Dion, from Louisiana, would likely say, "We goin to make groceries." It was clear to Mr. Drake that Black English varied by region, depending on the cultural context in which it was learned and used.

Mr. Drake thanked Ms. Manning for her comments.

On his way home from school, Mr. Drake wondered how he should respond to Matt's use of Black English in his paper.

Questions for Reflection

1. What other information, if any, would you need in order to decide how you would respond to Matt?
2. Write verbatim how you would begin a conversation with Matt about his use of Black English Vernacular. Include specific comments about how his use of BEV will affect his grade on this assignment and on other work in your class in the future.
3. How might your response affect Matt's learning, his sense of self-worth, and the socioemotional climate of your classroom?
4. What limits, if any, would you establish with respect to use of non–Standard English in your classroom?
5. How does the cultural context of the class, school, and community affect how you would respond to Matt?
6. What principles for grading and evaluation of oral and written language should a teacher use with students?

Activity for Extending Thinking

1. Discuss with parents and teachers, including parents and teachers of color, the issue of allowing/encouraging the use of dialects in the classroom. How flexible and responsive should a teacher be in accepting the use of dialects?

---

*Trudgill, P. (1984). Socio-linguistics: An introduction to language and society. New-York: Penguin Books, p. 20.

Case 24

*Values of Native American culture are introduced
through a small group activity that combines reading,
art design, and measuring.*

Here's What We'll Do . . .

It was Monday morning. Mr. Merritt had set up tables with equipment and supplies needed for his art project. Mr. Merritt told the students that they were going to make Navajo jewelry. They were going to make clay, design clay beads, and paint and string them together.

Mr. Merritt asked the class: "How many of you know what Navajo jewelry looks like?"

Sora replied, "When my family went to the Grand Canyon, we saw some Navajo jewelry."

Mr. Merritt prompted: "Could you tell us more?"

Sora shared several impressions about the trip and the jewelry. Mr. Merritt gave further information about the culture of the Navajo people and the design and production of Navajo necklaces.

Mr. Merritt then asked: "Has anyone ever read and followed a recipe before, or measured ingredients?" Several hands went up and at least half the children stated that they had helped their parents make some sort of dessert. Based on the children's experience and reading ability, Mr. Merritt divided them into groups of four.

Once the groups were at the tables, Mr. Merritt said, "I would like one team member to read the recipe for clay making, one member to measure the ingredients, one member to pour the ingredients into the bowl, and the fourth team member to mix it together. The person who reads the recipe will divide the clay into four equal parts. After that, you may start designing your beads." He paused while the members chose their jobs and then added, "If all of you finish the project by 11:30, we will have five minutes of free time before lunch. But don't rush; if you work steadily, you'll finish in plenty of time.

As the groups worked, Mr. Merritt circulated among them, reminding each student what he expected of that student and encouraging each to do his or her best. Students seemed to accept his challenges for learning.

Questions for Reflection

1. What aspects of Mr. Merritt's directions and procedures were communicated clearly? What suggestions would you make to improve the clarity of his directions? (Consider amount of detail, precision, transitions, and emphasis of his communication.)
2. Have you had experience with this type of small group, hands-on lesson? If so, what are the essential ingredients that contribute to the success (or failure) of such a lesson?
3. What related lessons might you use prior to or following Mr. Merritt's lesson to include higher levels of multicultural curriculum, according to the Banks model (see Appendix B).
4. When communicating with students in the classroom, to what degree is it necessary to (a) reinforce oral directions and instructions with written ones and (b) model the use of formal versus informal speech?

Activities for Extending Thinking

1. Some scholars define "clear" communication as that which is precise, has smooth transitions, and emphasizes the more important parts of the message. Think of an activity or set of classroom procedures that you might communicate to students. Write out the instructions/directions for the activity. Finally, analyze your written statement to see if it is precise, has smooth transitions, and emphasizes the most important aspects of the activity. A colleague who teaches at the same grade level can aid your analysis.
2. Using a set of written instructions or directions for an activity that you have used in the past, perform the same analysis as described in activity 1.

Case 25

*A teacher responds to a student's apprehension
about giving his first oral report to the class.*

What If I Can't Get
Their Attention?

Mr. Bailey wanted his students to become more confident speakers. He had given his class extensive written directions on designing and presenting an oral report. The primary goals of the activity were twofold (1) to learn and practice presentation skills and (2) to teach the class about some of the values of another cultural group. Students were to select a cultural group that was part of their own heritage.

Several days before the presentation, Qui, a shy Cambodian student, privately expressed concerns about being able to help keep the class interested during his report. Mr. Bailey reviewed several specific presentation skills on the board.

Qui: I understand what you said about hand gestures, talking louder and softer, and looking at students, but what about the kids who aren't watching?

Mr. Bailey: Continue with your movements, changes in voice, and random eye contact. Don't stare at one or two of your classmates. You may make them nervous.

Qui: What if I can't get their attention?

Mr. Bailey: I understand how you feel, Qui. I remember the first report I gave. I thought everyone was bored out of their minds. But, I concentrated on my material and found a friendly face once in a while among my classmates and I did all right. Feeling relaxed in front of many people is difficult, but with practice and a couple of smiles and nods from me you'll be fine. I'm sure they'll find your report very interesting—I know I want to learn more about the things you and your family consider important. And they'll really love the artwork you're bringing!

Qui: I'll do my best, Mr. Bailey.

Mr. Bailey: You'll feel better if you practice at home in front of a mirror tonight. Will you do that for me?

Qui: Yes

Mr. Bailey: See you tomorrow.

Questions for Reflection

1. Was Mr. Bailey's strategy for engagement (student reports) appropriate for the learning goals he had set? What alternate strategy(ies) might he have used?
2. Following is a list of elements that can foster student engagement.* Comment on the form in which each element was present in Mr. Baily's student report strategy. Also rate the effectiveness of the element in helping students engage in the lesson.

Element	Form[†]	Effectiveness
a. Presentation of content (oral, visual, discussion, laboratory, etc.)		low 1 2 3 4 5 high
b. Emphasis on problem solving		1 2 3 4 5
c. Provision for student choice and initiative		1 2 3 4 5
d. Emphasis on depth rather than breadth		1 2 3 4 5
e. Requiring student thinking		1 2 3 4 5
f. Relevance and authenticity		1 2 3 4 5
g. Grouping of students		1 2 3 4 5
h. Use of instructional materials and resources		1 2 3 4 5
i. Structure and pacing		1 2 3 4 5

[†]The way that the element was included

3. Assess the adequacy of Mr. Bailey's response to Qui.
4. What, if any, adjustments in the lesson should he have made in light of Qui's concerns?

Activity for Extending Thinking

1. Discuss with practicing teachers their methods for engaging students in learning, including the most successful types of (a) activities and assignments, (b) structure and pacing of lessons, (c) grouping of students, and (d) favorite kinds of instructional

*The list of elements is based on Danielson, C. (1996). *Enhancing professional practice: A framework for teaching* (pp. 96-97). Alexandria, VA: Association for Supervision and Curriculum Development.

materials and resources. Summarize your insights in writing and be prepared to share in class.

Case 26

A teacher finds herself repeatedly attending to disruptive students during the video hour each Friday.

Friday Is Video Day

It was Friday and Ms. Hanson loaded the videotape on the Apollo space project into the videocassette recorder. It was her opinion that if the students worked hard all week, they should be rewarded with a video on Friday. In addition to serving as a reward, the videos also varied the stimulus. Furthermore, they could engage students in constructing meaningful understandings of important concepts in science.

Students who were not interested in a particular video had the option of working on an extra credit project related to the current unit of study. This month the unit was on mass and volume. On this particular Friday, Jenny, Teresa, Angie, and Ann had opted to do extra credit rather than watch the tape. In fact, the same group had opted to do extra credit for the past three weeks.

This Friday was no different from other recent Fridays in that the group of four or five boys in the back of the room had again begun to talk during the video. For some reason, they always seemed to equate video watching with socializing.

To curb their talking, Ms. Hanson used proximity. Taking a seat next to the group allowed her to give them her full attention. From her vantage point, she could also see the students working on extra credit. If a student raised his or her hand for help, she could motion to the student to come to her. That way she could still remain close to the boys and keep their talking in check.

When Jenny and Ann raised their hands, Ms. Hanson waved them over. Jenny pointed to a problem at the end of the chapter, "I don't get number 8," she said. "Me either," added Ann.

"Let's take a look," replied Ms. Hanson. "What part do you understand?"

As Jenny began to respond, Ms. Hanson interrupted. "Hold that thought." She leaned toward Todd and Tim and with her finger to her lips said, "Shhh. Please, I've asked you before not to talk during the videos. Every time I have to come over here, it takes away from the time I could be helping someone." She waited several moments until the boys quieted down.

When she turned to Jenny, she apologized. "Sorry, where were we?" Jenny reminded her and they began again.

Later that hour, when Teresa sought help, Ms. Hanson had to again attend to the disruptive boys.

Later that day, on the way home from school, Ms. Hanson wondered about the Friday arrangement. She could not help noticing the patterns of behavior so typical of Fridays, including having to spend much of the period with the boys in the back of the room. She listed the pros: giving the student choices (to view the video or do extra credit), varying the stimulus, rewarding hard work, and giving personal attention to those who need it. Maybe the Friday arrangement was satisfactory after all.

Questions for Reflection

1. Respond to Ms. Hanson's practice of maintaining Fridays as days that students could choose to either watch an educational video or complete extra credit work. Do you agree or disagree with this practice? Why?
2. If you would change her Friday video activity, how would you do so? Give a rationale for any changes you would suggest. Consider the elements listed in the "Questions for Reflection" in the case prior to this one—which elements appear to be addressed effectively; which ones do not appear to be addressed effectively?
3. As noted in the introduction to this book, case-based or problem-based learning has high potential for engaging students in learning. Comment on how you might use cases to engage students in your classes.
4. What moral/ethical issues, if any, are raised in this case?
5. What issues of diversity, if any, are raised in this case?

Activities for Extending Thinking

1. Design a student survey that would elicit pupil opinion on the use of a particular activity such as the "video day" activity. What questions would you ask?
2. List two or three ideas around which you could develop cases (stories with problems) that you could use in classes you might teach. Begin by listing the key information you would want students to obtain or develop, and then briefly outline a story that would create in students the desire to obtain or construct that information.

Case 27

*After reading a story to his class, a teacher uses a variety of
questioning strategies to engage students in discussion.*

Dwight, What Do You Think?

Mr. Beach was beginning the third week of his first year of full-time
teaching. He had enjoyed the two years that he had been a substitute teacher, and he was excited about having his own class for the
first time.

Mr. Beach believed strongly in the need to develop a sense of
community in his class. During the first week of September, he had
the class learn and practice group membership skills, including
good listening skills. The students had demonstrated a high level of
proficiency in using the new skills, and they seemed to have begun
to feel a sense of unity as a class. In both large and small groups, students were cooperative with Mr. Beach and with one another.

Now, in the third week of school, the class was well into
reading *Love You Forever* by Robert Munsch. Mr. Beach's primary
goals were to have students (1) improve in reading comprehension
and (2) learn to enjoy reading, and he often began his lessons by
having students share previously acquired knowledge.

"Class," he said, "Tell me, does it appear that persons in the story
often used good listening skills when they were together?"

Several students raised their hands. Mr. Beach called on Dwight,
a bright-eyed African American student who sat in the front row.

"No," Dwight replied.

"What makes you say 'no'?" asked Mr. Beach.

Dwight appeared to be thinking.

After six or seven seconds, Mr. Beach asked, "What are the good
listening skills that we learned? Let's review."

Dwight replied, "Looking at the person—not staring though, not
interrupting, and being able to say what the person said."

"Excellent!" said Mr. Beach. "Now, did the little boy who grew up
to be a man use these kinds of skills as far as we can determine from
the story?"

"Yes," replied Dwight. "Cause he was able to say 'I'll love you forever' to his mother when she got old, so he must have listened to it
when he was growing up."

"Exactly," said Mr. Beach. "Now, class, why couldn't his mother
finish the saying when she was old? Mary?"

Mary thought a couple of seconds and then answered, "I'm not sure."

"Dara, what do you think?" asked Mr. Beach.

"Cause she was too old," answered Dara.

"Mahmoud, what what would you add to Dara's answer?"

Mahmoud responded, "Well, she was sick too."

"Yes, and when people get sick they get weak, don't they; sometimes too weak to talk, right?" asked Mr. Beach. Looking at Mahmoud, Mr. Beach continued, "Have you known anyone who was old and sick and almost too weak to talk?"

Mahmoud proceeded to tell the class about his grandfather who had been ill for several weeks with the flu and had to be hospitalized.

Several other students mentioned persons they had known who had been ill. They talked of being sad when their loved one was ill. The discussion continued to engage the students. They completely lost track of time. Mr. Beach was pleased about the students' understanding of the story, as well as their ability to connect to prior learning. Moreover, he was pleased with his ability to lead a good, lively, and productive discussion.

Questions for Reflection

1. Assume that the teacher's interaction as described in this case is typical of his interaction with students in his class. Assess his proficiency at using discussion and questioning techniques:

    What, if anything, did he do well? What positive effects did each action have on students?

    What, if anything, did he do that you would not recommend? Specifically, how (if at all) should he change his approach?
2. List any issues of cultural diversity embedded in this case. What should teachers do to address each issue?
3. Are there any moral/ethical issues embedded in this case? If so, how would you handle each of them?

Activity for Extending Thinking

1. What strategies or techniques for leading discussions are supported by research? Review research on discussion techniques, including skills/strategies such as
    a. Open-ended questions
    b. Inductive skills, such as comparing
    c. Deductive skills, such as suggesting a cause for observations made
    d. Hypothetical reasoning

e. Generalizing
f. Identifying goals
g. Using wait-time
h. Broadening participation
i. Listening and acknowledging student ideas
j. Closing discussions
k. Reflecting on discussions

Designing Your Own Case Instruction

Design a case related to classroom instruction. The story can focus on a method or strategy related to a single subject matter area (e.g., English or social studies) or on a more generic method or strategy pertinent to a wider range of subject matter areas. Some examples are

- Communicating clearly and accurately
- Using questioning and discussion techniques
- Engaging students in learning
- Grouping of students
- Providing feedback to students
- Demonstrating flexibility and responsiveness*

In selecting a topic, reflect on recent or current field experiences, personal experiences as a student, or accounts of real classroom incidents. Include some demographic data that tell a bit about the community, school, classroom, teacher, students, and curriculum. Include at least one problem to which there is no obvious answer. Use fictitious names of persons and schools to maintain confidentiality.

Your case should be approximately two pages in length (typed, double-spaced) and should include three to four Questions for Reflection and one to two Activities for Extending Thinking. A form entitled "Designing Your Own Case" is provided on the following two pages. It outlines categories for developing your case as well as for developing criteria for assessing responses to your Questions for Reflection and your Activities for Extending Thinking.

---

*Danielson, C. (1996). *Enhancing professional practice: A framework for teaching.* Alexandria, VA: Association for Supervision and Curriculum Development.

Designing Your Own Case

Author Name(s): _____

Title of Case: _____ Grade Level(s): _____

Subject Matter Area (e.g., science)_____ (OR)

    Generic Teaching Topic (e.g., grouping of students, questioning techniques): _____

_____

Contextual Information: _____

    Community factors: _____

    School factors: _____

    Classroom factors: _____

        Teacher characteristics: _____

        Student characteristics: _____

        Characteristics of curriculum: _____

Story: _____

_____

_____

_____

_____

Questions for Reflection:

1. _____

2. _____

3. _____

Activities for Extending Thinking:

1. _____

2. _____

Primary issue embedded in case (e.g., grouping of students, communicating clearly):

_____

_____

Secondary issues(e.g., diversity in education, gender equity):_____

_____

_____

Criteria for assessing responses to your Questions for Reflection:

List criteria (e.g., response is clear, consistent with research or best practice, generalized to an appropriate degree—not overgeneralized, valid—based on facts in the case, relevant to an issue in the case, other):

1. _____

2. _____

3. _____

Responses to Questions for Reflection:

List what you would consider to be examples of acceptable and unacceptable responses.

Acceptable	**Unacceptable**
1. a._____	_____
b._____	_____
2. a._____	_____
b._____	_____
3. a._____	_____
b._____	_____

Responses to Activities for Extended Thinking:

List examples of acceptable and unacceptable responses:

1. _____   _____

2. _____   _____

Suggested Readings

Brandt, R. (1992). On research on teaching: A conversation with Lee Shulman. *Educational Leadership, 49* (7), 14-19.

Brandt, R. (1994). On making sense: A conversation with Magdalene Lampert. *Educational Leadership, 51* (5), 26-30.

Brophy, J. E., & Good, T. L. (1986). Teacher behavior and student achievement. In M. C. Wittrock (Ed.), *Handbook of Research on Teaching* (3rd ed., pp. 328-375). New York: Macmillan.

Carter, K., Cushing, K., Sabers, D., Stein, P., & Berliner, D. (1988). Expert-novice differences in perceiving and processing visual classroom information. *Journal of Teacher Education, 39* (1), 25-31.

Cohen, D. K., McLaughlin, M. W., & Talbert, J. E. (Eds.). (1993). *Teaching for understanding: Challenges for policy and practice.* San Francisco: Jossey-Bass.

Edmonds, R., & Frederickson, N. (1978) *Search for effective schools: The identification and analysis of city schools that are instructionally effective for poor children.* Cambridge, MA: Harvard University Center for Policy Studies.

Ellett, C. (1990). *A new generation of classroom-based assessments of teaching and learning: Concepts, issues and controversies from pilots of the Louisiana STAR.* Baton Rouge: College of Education, Louisiana State University.

Gardner, H., & Boix-Mansilla, V. (1994). Teaching for understanding—within and across the disciplines. *Educational Leadership, 51*(5), 14-18.

Goodwin, S. S., Sharp, G. W., Cloutier, E. F., & Diamond, N. A. (1983). *Effective classroom questioning.* Paper identified by the Task Force on Establishing a National Clearinghouse of Materials Developed for Teaching Assistant (TA) Training. (ERIC Document Reproduction Service No. ED 235-497).

Heckman, P. E. (1994). Planting seeds: Understanding through investigation. *Educational Leadership, 51*(5), 36-39.

Joyce, B., & Weil, M. (1996). *Models of teaching.* Needham Heights, MA: Allyn & Bacon.

National Board for Professional Teaching Standards. (1991). *Toward high and rigorous standards for the teaching profession* (3rd ed.). Detroit: Author.

Nias, J., Southworth, G., & Campbell, P. (1992). *Whole school curriculum development in the primary school.* London: The Falmer Press.

Perkins, D., & Blythe, T. (1994). Putting understanding up front. *Educational Leadership, 51*(5), 4-7.

Perrone, V. (1994). How to engage students in learning. *Educational Leadership, 51*(5), 11-13.

Reynolds, A. (1992). What is competent beginning teaching? A review of the literature. *Review of Educational Research, 62*(1), 1-35.

Shulman, L. S. (1987). Knowledge and teaching: Foundations of the new reform. *Harvard Educational Review, 57*(1), 1-22.

U. S. Department of Education. (1987). *What works: Research about teaching and learning.* Washington, DC: U.S. Government Printing Office.

Williams, P. S. (1988). Going west to get east: Using metaphors as instructional tools. *Journal of Children in Contemporary Society, 20*(1-2), 79-98.

Wiske, M. S. (1994). How teaching for understanding changes the rules in the classroom. *Educational Leadership, 51*(5), 19-21.

Wolk, S. (1994). Project-based learning: Pursuits with a purpose. *Educational Leadership, 52*(3), 42-45.

Woods, R. K. (1994). A close-up look at how children learn science. *Educational Leadership, 51*(5), 33-35.

Zigmond, N., Sansone, J., Miller, S., Donahoe, K., & Kohnke, R. (1986). Teaching learning disabled students at the secondary school level: What research says to teachers. *Learning Disabilities Focus, 1*(2), 108-115.

Part 5
Professional Responsibilities

Creating Additional Context for a Given Case

Each case in this section is sufficiently complex to allow for multiple levels of analysis and multiple interpretations. Even so, it is important to bring your own knowledge and personal purpose to the analysis of a given case. Hence, the context within each case has purposely not been highly prescribed. For example, most of the cases purposely do not indicate the grade level, thereby allowing for a variety of readers to bring their own grade-level context to the case.

Therefore, as suggested in the introduction, prior to analyzing a given case, you are invited to modify its context. Your instructor will help decide which cases might be modified and the extent of the modifications and will direct you to do so individually, in small groups, or as a class.

When so directed by your instructor, include factors that make the case richer, more authentic, or more personally meaningful to you, your small group, or your class. You may want to re-create a context that resembles a school in which you are currently completing a field experience or in which you are teaching, or you may want to create a setting representing the type of school that you hope to work in some day. Include one or two factors from the following categories:

> *Characteristics of the community. You might include such factors as proportion of socioeconomic, ethnic, and religious groups and the sociopolitical attitudes of various community groups.*

> *Characteristics of the school. You might include demographics related to the ethnic, religious, and special needs make-up of the student body; curricular and extracurricular emphases of the school; and recent school reform efforts.*

> *Nature of the characters and the classroom. You might include information such as personal characteristics (e.g., physical appearance, social abilities, mannerisms and behavioral habits, intellectual abilities, and teaching or learning styles) or grade level of the class, physical arrangement of the classroom, type of curriculum, and daily schedule of the classes.*

For those cases identified by your instructor for analysis and for context modification, take a few minutes prior to analysis to list in writing several additional contextual variables that you believe are important.

Case 28

Students extend and refine reading and writing skills as they engage in a "social action" activity.

Let's Ask the Company to Change It

Mr. Hultgren's class had been keeping a record of upcoming class events, such as field trips, student report days, community service days, quizzes, and the like, on a commercial calendar. The pictures on the calendar were of children and adolescents—mostly close-ups showing facial expressions of wonder, excitement, happiness, and awe.

On the first day of November, Mr. Hultgren turned the page of the calendar. He began to review highlights of the field trip, report days, and tests for the month. Hector, an energetic youngster of Hispanic heritage, asked his teacher: "Mr. Hultgren, how come none of the pictures on the calendar have any kids that look like me?" Other students of color chimed in: "Yeah, or me?"

Mr. Hultgren's curriculum had a strong social justice orientation. In fact, his class monitored the school and the community newspapers to ensure proper treatment of traditionally underrepresented groups. However, he had not paid any attention to the pictures on this particular calendar. "You're right," he replied, looking through the rest of the pages. "There are no children of color in the remaining pictures, either. Can anyone think of anything we could do about this?"

"We could take some pictures of our class and other students in school and use those pictures instead of the ones in the calendar," Mia suggested. "That's a good idea," said Mr. Hultgren. "Any other ideas?"

Marty offered a suggestion: "Perhaps we can write to the publisher and ask them to add some children of color in their next one." The class agreed that it would be the right thing to do.

Mr. Hultgren designed some activities that included prewriting, editing, rewriting, spelling, grammar and usage, and business letter formatting. For the next week, students designed, edited, and revised a class letter to the calendar company. The letter was sent on Friday.

Five weeks later, the class received a letter from the calendar company. It said, "Thank you for making us aware of an oversight. We plan to add students of color to the calendar next year."

Questions for Reflection

1. What were the strengths of Mr. Hultgren's response to the calendar problem? What else would you have done?
2. List the specific behaviors that
   a. Demonstrated teacher and student efficacy
   b. Demonstrated that the teacher was an advocate for students' best interests
3. Describe any similar experiences you have had, that is, incidents in which students have taken a social action approach to solve a real problem in the school or broader community (see the "Social Action" approach in the Banks model, Appendix B).
4. Identify two student activities (like the one in the story) that would advocate for students and have the potential for improvements for traditionally oppressed groups.

Activities for Extending Thinking

1. Explore resources for students on the Internet. Identify ways that, as a professional, you can improve existing Internet resources and/or the development of new ones.
2. If you are in a field experience or if you are a practicing teacher, volunteer to participate in activities that serve students (e.g., special needs, bilingual programs, extracurricular activities). Keep a journal of key insights from your work.

Case 29

Several teachers discuss the difficulty of getting parents involved in school; one suggests an approach that worked for him.

Your Child Is So Good at—

It was lunch hour in the faculty lounge. Mr. Jordan said to the other five teachers at his table, "I was disappointed with the turnout at parent conferences last night. Only four parents attended. How many came to your conferences?" he asked.

The other teachers reported low numbers also. "The kids deserve more," one of them commented.

"I've tried everything to get parents to become more involved in the education of their children. I've had little success," said Mr. Jordan. "Have any of you found ways to reach parents?"

Several of the teachers described the ways in which they had tried, without success, to get parents to volunteer to assist with classes, help their own children with homework, attend school events, or come to parent conferences. One teacher had even offered to hold parent conferences in the lobby or conference room of the buildings in which a number of his students lived; still, few came.

Finally, Mr. Randall, a third grade teacher, spoke up: "For the first year ever, I have more parent volunteers to speak to my class, tutor, and act as a teacher's aide than I'll ever be able to use. It's really amazing!"

"Well," asked the others, "how did you do it?"

Mr. Randall responded, "This year, for the first time, I made certain that the first communication that each parent received from me was about some talent, gift, ability, or contribution that his or her child had made to class. I assumed that a positive response on my part would bring a positive response from parents, but I never imagined the response would be so overwhelming! I guess some parents may well have had negative experiences when they were in school and hence probably aren't eager to be involved with education. Sharing positive comments about their children helped them to feel accepted. In turn, they were willing to reciprocate."

Mr. Jordan wondered to himself if Mr. Randall's strategy would work for him. He thought to himself, "I'm not sure that just sending letters making positive comments about students could create such a favorable parental attitude. Is it possible?"

Questions for Reflection

1. Do you believe that Mr. Randall's strategy could work for other teachers? Why or why not?
2. What other strategies might be used to enhance communication with famlies?
3. What evidence from practice or research suggests that parent involvement has an impact on a child's academic success?
4. What are the greatest obstacles that keep families from participating in schools?
5. Some parents doubt the value of schooling as a path by which their children might gain access to cultural capital. How would you persuade them of the value of education for their children?

Activities for Extending Thinking

1. Interview parents of at least two students of a culture other than the dominant culture regarding their views on schooling. Elicit their thoughts and feelings on the (a) availability of information about curriculum, (b) availability of information from the school on their own children, and (c) engagement of families in the instructional program. Be prepared to summarize your insights in class.
2. As in activity 1, interview at least two parents of students of the dominant culture. Compare and contrast your findings for activities 1 and 2.

Case 30

A teacher explores new resources for helping students improve in reading and at the same time unexpectedly finds opportunities for her own professional development.

Professional Growth and Instructional Support

Ms. King was in her third year of teaching. She was confident about her knowledge of her subject matter areas, her ability to develop thematic curriculum, and her skills for developing rapport with students. She was a skilled facilitator of learning and an effective classroom manager.

For the second year in a row, however, Ms. King had noted a significant increase in the number of students who had difficulty reading. On the one hand, she believed that the ability to read was crucial for students, for it could limit or enhance their chances for success in all subject matter areas. On the other hand, she was not an expert in reading improvement and was becoming increasingly frustrated with her ability to help students become better readers.

The school reading specialist, burdened with developmental, recreational, and enrichment reading programs, offered ideas to Ms. King and the other teachers, but time constraints disallowed systematic help for improving reading in the content areas. Ms. King was not sure where to turn.

At the next faculty meeting at her school, a professor of education from a nearby college was present. He had been asked by the principal to invite ideas for developing programs of mutual benefit to Ms. King's school and his college. He distributed an interest assessment survey on which faculty members were to list programs of interest. When he talked of the possibility of having a college student pair with a pupil from the school and communicate via e-mail (as well as in person), Ms. King got an idea. Knowing that her students needed help with reading, she decided to make a proposal to Dr. Watson.

After the meeting Ms. King approached the visitor. "Dr. Watson," she began, "do you have a minute?"

"Why yes," he replied, extending his hand in greeting. "Nice to meet you. What can I do for you?"

"My name is Ms. King," she began and then told him of her concern about the low reading scores of students and asked if there might be some way in which the college could help. "One thing I could really use would be reading 'buddies' or tutors for my students. I have a number of limited English proficiency students, mostly of Latino and Hmong heritage, who could use some help. Of course, all the students could benefit from reading buddies," she concluded.

Dr. Watson brightened: "Actually, I have an idea that may work. I teach a class in which my students are to develop skills and strategies for helping elementary school students become better readers. We could set up a clinical experience in which they would work with the kinds of students they will one day teach."

He continued, "I normally have 20 education students per term, and it would be reasonable to require one hour of reading tutoring per week for 10 weeks. They could meet some of those weeks at your school, and other weeks on our college campus, if possible. How would that work for you?"

"That would be wonderful!" Ms. King replied. "In fact," she said, "we could even give the students a measure of their reading ability before the tutoring program and again after it to see what effects, if any, it had. I'm sure that others on the faculty, as well as Ms. Arndt, our principal, would be interested. If the results are significant, the program could be expanded."

Dr. Watson nodded in agreement, "I think that's an excellent idea! When would you like to begin?"

"The sooner the better," Ms. King replied. "Could we meet and discuss this matter further?"

"I'd be delighted," said Dr. Watson. "I'll call you tomorrow—what time is best?"

Ms. King identified her preparation period and wrote down her phone number. "I look forward to your call!" she said.

As she headed back toward her room, she thought to herself that developing a new, low-cost program to help students become better readers would be a dream come true. And conducting action research in her classroom and making the results known to colleagues was frosting on the cake!

Questions for Reflection

1. Although Ms. King's newfound resource has potential, a number of issues need to be worked out. List the most important issues and how you would address each as a teacher.

Issue	Method of Addressing
a.	a.
b.	b.
c.	c.

2. What suggestions other than a tutoring program with college students might you have to help Ms. King's students improve their reading?
3. Ms. King saw an opportunity to help her students while at the same time learning and growing herself as she conducted research and took a leadership role in program development in the school. What other examples of conducting research and/or taking a leadership role in the school have you observed?
4. What goals for professional development might you have? What resources will be required in order for you to attain those goals? What are the next steps in the process of goal attainment?

Activities for Extending Thinking

1. Discuss with several teachers (in your field experience school or the school in which you work) their professional development achievements within the past few years. Be prepared to summarize your insights in class.
2. Interview at least one school administrator about district support for professional development opportunities for teachers in his or her district.

Case 31

*Designing, maintaining, and using records become
topics of discussion between two teachers.*

Records, Portfolios,
and Computers

Ms. Bonilla loved teaching. She had been in business for 10 years previously, and she liked to remind her colleagues how grateful she was for the chance to return to college to acquire a teaching license.

Perhaps the least-liked aspects of teaching for Ms. Bonilla were keeping detailed records on students' academic progress and noninstructional activities such as permission slips for field trips, attendance forms, and the like. She kept the records, but she would rather plan, implement, and evaluate student learning. She loved interacting with young people, particularly when she could see the rewards of helping them learn and grow.

In terms of developing, maintaining, and using academic records, her biggest concern came at the end of the term when she had to convert her grades for assignments to a term grade. Specifically, she was uncomfortable with the school practice that required her to convert a single cumulative grade from assignments to term grades for (1) achievement, (2) attitude, and (3) effort. She also gave attendance and behavioral conduct "grades," but those were usually more straightforward.

After school one day, she explained the problem to Mr. Elway, a colleague who taught in the classroom next to hers. "My problem is this," she began, "I'm asked to assign a grade for each academic task, for example, for each project that students complete. I give each task "1," "2," or "3." At the end of the term, I total all of those grades for each student. Let's say a given student has earned an average of "2" for all academic tasks. Now, on the school report card, I'm required to convert that single grade of "2" to one grade for achievement, one for attitude, and a third for effort. It's hard to separate one grade into three! I'm not sure I'm being fair to all the students."

Mr. Elway concurred: "I've had the same problem. I'd like to have a broader base for grading from the start of the year. I'm experimenting with requiring portfolios for students, and that should help. In addition to having a wider range of items to judge, I'll grade each task on (1) overall quality, (2) promptness, and (3) the amount of effort given by the student. Then at the end of the term, I won't have to break one grade into three. It will literally triple my record-keeping burden—that's the part I don't like! But I do think it will be more accurate and fair for the students."

"That sounds like an interesting plan," replied Ms. Bonilla. "Could I see the forms that you use?"

"Sure, I'll make a copy for you by tomorrow. I'll put them in your mailbox," Mr. Elway said as he smiled.

"Oh, one last question," added Ms. Bonilla. "I heard that you allow your students to keep electronic portfolios—stored on the computer. Could you show me that?"

Mr. Elway responded, "I'd be happy to show you. I need to get ready for class right now, but let's talk at lunch."

Ms. Bonilla thanked him as he left. She was indeed appreciative of the collegial relationship that she had with Mr. Elway, and for that matter, with the other teachers in the school.

Questions for Reflection

1. How would you respond to Ms. Bonilla's concern about dividing the single end-of-the-term grade into three grades?
2. What do you like about Mr. Elway's approach to keeping records of all three grades throughout the term? What do you dislike about it?
3. What related problems have you experienced or do you anticipate in keeping records of student progress for noninstructional activities (e.g., collecting milk money, creating supply orders, obtaining permission slips for field trips)?
4. How could portfolios be used to gather information on (a) quality of work, (b) timeliness of work, and (c) student effort? What items would you include in a portfolio?
5. What computer programs exist for simplifying the record-keeping responsibilities of teachers? Which programs would you recommend as being the easiest to use, the most accurate, and the most cost effective?
6. Ms. Bonilla seemed to have a good collegial relationship with Mr. Elway. What can schools do to encourage positive professional relationships among staff? What can individual teachers do?

Activities for Extending Thinking

1. Interview a practicing teacher who uses an electronic grade-book or electronic portfolio program to record student progress in learning. Ask for a hands-on demonstration if possible. List the

advantages and limitations of this system and be prepared to summarize in class.

2. Discuss with an administrator, a parent, a student, and a teacher how grades are reported (e.g., the contents of the report card), and any changes they would like to see in this procedure. Summarize your findings in writing and be prepared to share in class.

Case 32

A teacher finds it difficult to supervise a student teacher during a term in which he has major coaching responsibilities and pressing family obligations.

I'd Rather Not Supervise a Student Teacher This Term

If there was a faculty team meeting, it must be Thursday. Each week without fail, teams would meet to discuss curriculum, budget, assessment, parent involvement, or other issues of concern. Mr. Casey looked at his agenda. It read: "assignment of student teachers."

Ms. Munson, the lead teacher, opened the meeting. After approval of the agenda of the previous meeting, she announced that a local college had offered to provide two student teachers for the coming term. She reminded the faculty that it was Mr. Casey's and Mr. Popp's turn to supervise a student teacher. Both knew that they were next in the rotation.

Mr. Casey asked if he could "pass" this term because he would be coaching and his wife was pregnant with their second child. "It will be a busy term for us," he said. "I'd be happy to take a turn in the spring."

Ms. Munson asked if anyone would offer to trade with Mr. Casey. No one did. All were tied up with site councils, curriculum review committees, the school play, or the designing of new performance assessment plans for their areas. Grudgingly, Mr. Casey accepted his assignment, "OK, but I'm not going to be able to give it my all." Ms. Munson handed him a slip of paper with his student teacher's name—Jon Porter—and phone number.

On the following Monday, Jon arrived in Mr. Casey's class. He observed for the first week and then began to teach one hour each day. Wanting to give Jon some freedom to get to know the students, Mr. Casey stayed out of the classroom. He made good use of his time planning team strategy.

On the day of the first visit of the college supervisor, Mr. Casey was out of school ill. The following week when the college supervisor came, Mr. Casey had to take his wife to the hospital to deliver their daughter. Finally, at mid-term, Mr. Casey and the college supervisor met to talk about Jon's performance.

"I've observed Jon several times, each time for at least a half hour. He's doing fine," said Mr. Casey. "He knows his material, he plans well, and the kids like him."

Dr. Walker, the college supervisor, asked, "Is he able to demonstrate that students are learning?"

Mr. Casey replied, "Why yes, they complete their worksheets, do well on quizzes, and when he asks them if there are any questions at the end of the period, they all indicate that they understand the material."

"And you're satisfied that that means they are learning?" asked Dr. Walker.

"Yes, I think so," said Mr. Casey.

"We like to have student teachers and cooperating teachers set specific, personal goals for improvement for the second half of the term. Could you and Jon write up a simple contract and have Jon make a copy for me?" asked Dr. Walker.

"Sure, we'll do it next week. Thanks for coming out today. I teach next hour and I really need to get ready. Perhaps we can talk longer next time. And I'll let you know if Jon has any problems," Mr. Casey promised as he showed Dr. Walker the door.

The next day, Mr. Casey asked Jon to set five specific personal goals for improvement. Jon submitted a set the following day. They read: "Use more higher-level questions; allow more wait time after asking a question; monitor distribution of leadership roles with special attention to gender bias; build student self-esteem through listening and acknowledging and through reinforcement; use more computer technology—Internet and CD-ROM programs—with the students."

Mr. Casey read the list: "These goals look good Jon. I'll keep a copy so that at the end of the term we can discuss if you've met them."

Because of his busy schedule, Mr. Casey could meet with Dr. Walker only one more time during the term.

Jon's classes generally went well during the second half of the term, with just the usual problems encountered by student teachers. For instance, some students seemed unsure of what they were to do on certain assignments, while others seemed less than fully engaged in the lesson. Mr. Casey's rating of Jon's work was "good" on a scale of "poor," "fair," "good," "very good," and "excellent."

Questions for Reflection

1. How would you rate Mr. Casey's performance as a student teacher supervisor? What, if anything, should Mr. Casey have done to contribute more to his student teacher's experience?

2. Should the lead teacher have been more supportive of Mr. Casey? What, if anything, should she have done differently?
3. What, if anything, should the college supervisor have done differently? Why?
4. What could Jon have done in this situation to improve his student teaching experience?
5. How should teachers document their contributions to the school and profession?

Activities for Extending Thinking

1. Discuss with an officer or leader of a local teachers' union the union's position on the role of the school, the college, and other players in the training of teachers.
2. Discuss with two experienced practicing teachers their views on participating in school and district events. Be prepared to share a summary of your insights with the class.

Designing Your Own Case
Professional Responsibilities

Design a case related to professional responsibilities. The story can focus on a method or strategy related to a single subject matter area (e.g., English or social studies) or on a more generic method or strategy pertinent to a wider range of subject matter areas. Some examples are

- Reflecting on teaching
- Maintaining accurate records
- Communicating with families
- Contributing to the school district
- Growing and developing professionally
- Showing Professionalism*

In selecting a topic, reflect on recent or current field experiences, personal experiences as a student, or accounts of real classroom incidents. Include some demographic data that tell a bit about the community, school, classroom, teacher, students, and curriculum. Include at least one problem to which there is no obvious answer. Use fictitious names of persons and schools to maintain confidentiality.

Your case should be approximately two pages in length (typed, double-spaced) and should include three to four Questions for Reflection and one to two Activities for Extending Thinking. A form entitled "Designing Your Own Case." is provided on the following pages. It outlines categories for developing your case as well as for developing criteria for assessing responses to your Questions for Reflection and your Activities for Extending Thinking.

---

*The examples are from Danielson, C. (1996). *Enhancing professional practice: A framework for teaching*. Alexandria, VA: Association for Supervision and Curriculum Development.

Designing Your Own Case

Author Name(s): _____

Title of Case: _____ Grade Level(s): _____

Subject Matter Area (e.g., science)_____ (OR)

    Generic Teaching Topic (e.g., reflecting on teaching, maintaining accurate records):

_____

Contextual Information: _____

    Community factors: _____

    School factors: _____

    Classroom factors: _____

        Teacher characteristics: _____

        Student characteristics: _____

        Characteristics of curriculum: _____

Story: _____

_____

_____

_____

_____

_____

_____

Questions for Reflection:

1. _____

2. _____

3. _____

Activities for Extending Thinking:

1. _____

2. _____

Primary issue embedded in case (e.g., reflecting on teaching, communicating with families):

_____

_____

107

Secondary issues(e.g., diversity in education, gender equity):_____

_____

_____

Criteria for assessing responses to your Questions for Reflection:

List criteria (e.g., response is clear, consistent with research or best practice, generalized to an appropriate degree—not overgeneralized, valid—based on facts in the case, relevant to an issue in the case, other):

1._____

2._____

3._____

Responses to Questions for Reflection:

List what you would consider to be examples of acceptable and unacceptable responses.

	Acceptable	**Unacceptable**
1. a.	_____	_____
b.	_____	_____
2. a.	_____	_____
b.	_____	_____
3. a.	_____	_____
b.	_____	_____

Responses to Activities for Extended Thinking:

List examples of acceptable and unacceptable responses:

1. _____   _____

2. _____   _____

Suggested Readings

Cruickshank, D. R. (1990). *Research that informs teachers and teacher educators.* Bloomington, IN: Phi Delta Kappa Educational Foundation.

Ellwein, M. C., Graue, M. E., & Comfort, R. E. (1990). Talking about instruction: Student teachers' reflections on success and failure in the classroom. *Journal of Teacher Education, 41*(4), 3–14.

Henderson, J. (1996). *Reflective teaching: The study of your constructivist practices.* Englewood Cliffs, NJ: Prentice Hall.

Hilliard, A. G. (1989, January). Teachers and cultural style in a pluralistic society. *NEA Today,* pp. 65–69.

National Board for Professional Teaching Standards. (1991). *Toward high and rigorous standards for the teaching profession* (3rd ed.). Detroit: Author.

Pajares, M. F. (1992). Teachers' beliefs and educational research: Cleaning up a messy act. *Review of Educational Research, 62*(3) 307–332.

Pitton, D. (1998). *Stories of student teaching: A case approach to the student teaching experience.* Upper Saddle River, NJ: Prentice Hall.

Porter, A. C., & Brophy, J. E. (1987, June). Good teaching: Insights from the work of the Institute for Research on Teaching. (Occasional Paper No. 114). East Lansing: The Institute for Research on Teaching, Michigan State University.

Porter, A. C., & Brophy, J. E. (1988). Synthesis of research on good teaching: Insights from the work of the Institute for Research on Teaching. *Educational Leadership, 45*(8), 74–85.

Powell, J. H., Casanova, U., & Berliner, D. C. (1991). *Parental involvement: Readings in educational research, a program for professional development, a National Education Association project.* Washington, DC: National Education Association.

Ross, J. A., & Regan, E. M. (1993). Sharing professional experience: Its impact on professional development. *Teaching and Teacher Education, 9*(1), 91–106.

Schön, D. (1987). *Educating the reflective practitioner: Toward a new design for teaching and learning in the professions.* San Francisco: Jossey-Bass.

Schunk, D. H. (1991). Self-efficacy and academic motivation. *Educational Psychologist, 26,* 207–231.

U.S. Department of Education. (1987). *What works: Research about teaching and learning.* Washington, DC: U.S. Government Printing Office.

Appendix A

The Four Domains of Teaching Responsibility[*]

Although teachers sometimes feel pulled in many different directions—at one moment, they are a counselor; at another, a business manager—a unifying thread runs through all their tasks to provide an organizing structure. That thread is engaging students in learning important content. All the components of the framework serve this primary purpose. And in pursuit of important learning, a teacher creates, with the students, a community of learners, in which all students feel respected and honored.

Each of the four domains of the framework for teaching refers to a distinct aspect of teaching. To some degree, the components within each domain form a coherent body of knowledge and skill, which can be the subject of focus independent of the other domains. Of course, there are many points of connection across domains. A teacher cannot demonstrate the highest level of skill in questioning and discussion techniques (Component 3b) if students do not feel the classroom environment is safe for taking risks and that their ideas will be respected (Component 2a). The following section describes each domain, identifies common themes that run through the components, and explains the concepts underlying the four levels of performance that are displayed by teachers of different levels of skills.

Domain 1: Planning and Preparation

The components in Domain 1 define how a teacher organizes the content that the students are to learn—how the teacher *designs* instruction (see "Components of Professional Practice," p. 115). All aspects of instructional planning are covered, beginning with a deep understanding of content and pedagogy and an understanding and appreciation of the students and what they bring to the educational encounter. But understanding the content is not sufficient. The content must be transformed through instructional design into sequences of activities and exercises that make it accessible to students. All elements of the

[*]Taken directly from Danielson, C. (1996). *Enhancing professional practice: A framework for teaching.* Alexandria, VA: Association for Supervision and Curriculum Development.

instructional design—learning activities, materials, and strategies—should be appropriate to both the content and the students. In their content and process, assessment techniques must also reflect the instructional goals and should serve to document student progress during and at the end of a teaching episode.

Teachers who excel in Domain 1 design instruction that reflects an understanding of content and important concepts and principles within that content. Their design is coherent in its approach to topics, includes sound assessment methods, and is appropriate to the range of students in the class. The instructional design, *as a design,* works.

Skills in Domain 1 are demonstrated primarily through the plans that teachers prepare to guide their teaching and ultimately through the success of those plans as implemented in the classroom. The plans may be included in a teacher's professional portfolio; the plan's effects must be observed through action in the classroom.

Domain 2: The Classroom Environment

Domain 2 consists of the interactions that occur in a classroom (see p. 115). The interactions are themselves noninstructional, even though they are necessary for effective instruction. Such activities and tasks establish a comfortable and respectful classroom environment, which cultivates a culture for learning and creates a safe place for risk taking. The atmosphere is businesslike, with noninstructional routines and procedures handled efficiently; student behavior is cooperative and nondisruptive; and the physical environment is supportive of the stated instructional purposes.

When students remember their teachers years later, it is often for the teachers' skill in Domain 2. Students recall the warmth and caring their favorite teachers demonstrated, the high expectations for achievement, and the teachers' commitment to their students. Students feel safe with these teachers' and know that they can count on them to be fair and, when necessary, compassionate.

Teachers who excel in Domain 2 consider their students as real people with interests, concerns, and intellectual potential. In return, the students regard them as concerned and caring adults and entrust the teachers with their futures. Such teachers never forget their proper role as adults, so they do not try to be pals. They also know that their natural authority with students is grounded in their knowledge and expertise rather than in their role alone. These teachers are indisputably in charge, but their students regard them as a special sort of friend, a protector, a challenger, someone who will permit no harm. As such, these teachers are remembered for years with appreciation.

Skills in Domain 2 are demonstrated through classroom interaction and captured on paper through interviews with or surveys of students. These skills must be observed in action, either in person or on videotape.

Domain 3: Instruction

Domain 3 contains the components that are at the fundamental heart of teaching—the actual engagement of students in content. It is impossible to overstate the importance of Domain 3 (see p. 116), which reflects the primary mission of schools: to enhance student learning. The components in Domain 3 are unified through the model of students' constructing meaning and participating in a community of learners. Domain 3 components represent distinct elements of instruction.

Teachers who excel in Domain 3 create an atmosphere of excitement about the importance of learning and the significance of the content. They care deeply about their subject and invite students to share the journey of learning about it. Students are engaged in meaningful work that carries significance beyond the next test and can provide skills and knowledge necessary for answering important questions or contributing to important projects. Such teachers do not have to motivate their students because the ways in which teachers organize and present the content, the roles they encourage students to assume, and the student initiative they expect serve to motivate students to excel. The work is real and significant, and it is important to students as well as to teachers.

Skills in Domain 3 are demonstrated through classroom interaction, either observed in person or videotaped.

Domain 4: Professional Responsibilities

The components in Domain 4 are associated with being a true professional educator. They encompass the roles assumed outside of and in addition to those in the classroom (see p. 116). Students rarely observe these activities; parents and the larger community observe them intermittently. But the activities are critical to preserving and enhancing the profession. Educators practice them primarily after their first few years of teaching, after they have mastered, to some degree, the details of classroom management and instruction.

Domain 4 consists of a wide range of professional responsibilities, from self-reflection and professional growth to contributions to the school and district and to the profession as a whole. The components also include interactions with the families of students, contacts with the larger community, the maintenance of records and other paperwork, and advocacy for students.

Teachers who excel in Domain 4 are highly regarded by colleagues and parents. They can be depended on to serve students' interests and the larger community, and they are active in their professional organizations, in the school, and in the district. They are known as educators who go beyond the technical requirements of their jobs and contribute to the general well-being of the institutions of which they are a part.

Skills in Domain 4 are demonstrated through teacher interactions with colleagues, families, other professionals, and the larger community. Some of these interactions may be documented in logs and placed in a portfolio. It is the interactions themselves, however, that must be observed to indicate a teacher's skill and commitment.

Figure 1 Components of Professional Practice

Domain 1: Planning and Preparation

Component 1a: Demonstrating Knowledge of Content and Pedagogy
Knowledge of content
Knowledge of prerequisite relationships
Knowledge of content-related pedagogy

Component 1b: Demonstrating Knowledge of Students
Knowledge of characteristics of age group
Knowledge of students' varied approaches to learning
Knowledge of students' skills and knowledge
Knowledge of students' interests and cultural heritage

Component 1c: Selecting Instructional Goals
Value
Clarity
Suitability for diverse students
Balance

Component 1d: Demonstrating Knowledge of Resources
Resources for teaching
Resources for students

Component 1e: Designing Coherent Instruction
Learning activities
Instructional materials and resources
Instructional groups
Lesson and unit structure

Component 1f: Assessing Student Learning
Congruence with instructional goals
Criteria and standards
Use for planning

Domain 2: The Classroom Environment

Component 2a: Creating an Environment of Respect and Rapport
Teacher interaction with students
Student interaction

Component 2b: Establishing a Culture for Learning
Importance of the content
Student pr de in work
Expectatio ns for learning and achievement

Component 2c: Managing Classroom Procedures
Management of instructional groups
Management of transitions
Management of materials and supplies
Performance of nonistructional duties
Supervision of volunteers and parapro-fessionals

Component 2d: Managing Student Behavior
Expectations
Monitoring of student behavior
Response to student misbehavior

Component 2e: Organizing Physical Space
Safety and arrangement of furniture
Accessibility to learning and use of physical resources

Continued

Figure I Components of Professional Practice (continued)

Domain 3: Instruction

Component 3a: *Communicating Clearly and Accurately*
Directions and procedures
Oral and written language

Component 3b: *Using Questioning and Discussion Techniques*
Quality of questions
Discussion techniques
Student participation

Component 3c: *Engaging Students in Learning*
Representation of content
Activities and assignments
Grouping of students
Instructional materials and resources
Structure and pacing

Component 3d: *Providing Feedback to Students*
Quality: accurate, substantive, constructive, and specific
timeliness

Component 3e: *Demonstrating Flexibility and Responsiveness*
Lesson adjustment
Response to students

Domain 4: Professional Responsibilities

Component 4a: *Reflecting on Teaching*
Accuracy
Use in future teaching

Component 4b: *Maintaining Accurate Records*
Student completion of assignments
Student progress in learning
Noninstructional records

Component 4c: *Communicating with Families*
Information about the instructional program
Information about individual students
Engagement of families in the instructional program

Component 4d: *Contributing to the School and District*
Relationships with colleagues
Service to the school
Participation in school and district projects

Component 4e: *Growing and Developing Professionally*
Enhancement of content knowledge and pedagogical skill
Service to the profession

Component 4f: *Showing Professionalism*
Service to students
Advocacy

From Danielson, C. (1996). *Enhancing professional practice: A framework for teaching.* Alexandria, VA: Association for Supervision and Curriculum Development, pp. 3–4.

Figure 2 Correlation of the INTASC Standards with the Framework for Teaching Components

INTASC Standard	Description of Teacher Performance	Framework Component	Description of Teacher Performance
Principle 1	Understands the central concepts, tools of inquiry, and structure of the disciplines taught; creates learning experiences to make them meaningful to students	1a 1e 3c	Demonstrates knowledge of content and pedagogy Designs coherent instruction Engages students in learning
Principle 2	Understands how children learn and develop; provides learning opportunities that support their development	1b 1c 1f 3b 3c	Demonstrates knowledge of students Selects instructional goals Assesses student learning Uses questioning and discussion techniques Engages students in learning
Principle 3	Understands how students differ in their approaches to learning; creates instructional opportunities adapted to diverse learners	1b 1e 2a 2b 3b to 3 e	Demonstrates knowledge of students Designs coherent instruction Creates an environment of respect and rapport Establishes a culture of learning Instruction Domain.
Principle 4	Understands and uses variety of instructional strategies	1d 1e 3b to 3e	Demonstrates knowledge of resources Designs coherent instruction Instruction Domain
Principle 5	Creates learning environment that encourages positive social interaction, active engagement in learning, and self-motivation	1e 2a 2b 2c 2d 2e 3c	Designs coherent instruction Creates an environment of respect and rapport Establishes a culture for learning Manages classroom procedures Manages student behavior Organizes physical space Engages students in learning

Figure 2 Correlation of the INTASC Standards with the Framework for Teaching Components (continued)

INTASC Standard	Description of Teacher Performance	Framework Component	Description of Teacher Performance
Principle 6	Uses knowledge of communication techniques to foster active inquiry, collaboration, and supportive interaction	2a 3a 3b 3c	Creates an environment of respect and rapport Communicates clearly and accurately Uses questioning and discussion techniques Engages students in learning
Principle 7	Plans instruction based on knowledge of subject matter, students, the community, and curriculum goals	1a to 1e 3c 3e	Planning and Preparation Domain Engages students in learning Demonstrates flexibility and responsiveness
Principle 8	Understands and uses formal and informal assessment strategies	1b 1f 3d 3e 4a 4b 4c	Demonstrates knowledge of students Assesses student learning Provides feedback to students Demonstrates flexibility and responsiveness Reflects on teaching Maintains accurate records Communicates with families
Principle 9	Reflects on teaching	4a 4d 4e	Reflects on teaching Contributes to the school and district Grows and develops professionally
Principle 10	Fosters relationships with colleagues, parents, and agencies in the larger community	1d 4c 4d 4f	Demonstrates knowledge of resources Communicates with families Contributes to the school and district Shows professionalism

From Danielson, C. (1996). *Enhancing professional practice: A framework for teaching.* Alexandria, VA: Association for Supervision and Curriculum Development, pp. 10–11.

Appendix B

Banks's Approaches for the Integration of Multicultural Content[*]

Approach	Description	Examples	Strengths	Problems
Contributions	Heroes, cultural components, holidays, and other discrete elements related to ethnic groups are added to the curriculum on special days, occasions, and celebrations.	Famous Mexican Americans are studied only during the week of Cinco de Maya (May 5). African Americans are studied during African American History Month in February but rarely during the rest of the year. Ethnic foods are studied in the first grade with little attention devoted to the cultures in which the foods are embedded.	Provides a quick and relatively easy way to put ethnic content into the curriculum. Gives ethnic heroes visibility in the curriculum alongside mainstream heroes. Is a popular approach among teachers and educators.	Results in a superficial understanding of ethnic cultures. Focuses on the lifestyles and artifacts of ethnic groups and reinforces stereotypes and misconceptions. Mainstream criteria are used to select heroes and cultural elements for inclusion in the curriculum.
Additive	This approach consists of the addition of content, concepts, themes, and perspectives to the curriculum without changing its structures.	Adding the book The Color Purple to a literature unit without reconceptualizing the unit or giving the students the background knowledge to understand the book. Adding a unit on the Japanese American internment to a U.S. history course without treating the Japanese in any other unit. Leaving the core curriculum intact but adding an ethnic studies course as an elective that focuses on a specific ethnic group.	Makes it possible to add ethnic content to the curriculum without changing its structure, which requires substantial curriculum changes and staff development. Can be implemented within the existing curriculum structure.	Reinforces the idea that ethnic history and culture are not integral parts of U.S. mainstream culture. Students view ethnic groups from Anglocentric and Eurocentric perspectives. Fails to help students understand how the dominant culture and ethnic cultures are inter-connected and interrelated.

[*]Banks, J. A. Approaches to cultural curriculum reform. In Banks, J. A., & Banks, C. A. M. (Eds.). (1997). *Multicultural education: Issues and perspectives* (pp. 229–250). Boston: Allyn & Bacon .

Banks's Approaches for the Integration of Multicultural Content (cont)

Approach	Description	Examples	Strengths	Problems
Transformation	The basic goals, structure, and nature of the curriculum are changed to enable students to view concepts, events, issues, problems, and themes from the perspectives of diverse cultural, ethnic, and racial groups.	A unit on the American Revolution describes the meaning of the revolution to Anglo revolutionaries, Anglo loyalists, African Americans, Indians, and the British. A unit on 20th century U.S. literature includes works by William Faulkner, Joyce Carol Oates, Langston Hughes, N. Scott Momoday, Saul Bellow, Maxine Hong Kingston, Rudolfo A. Anaya, and Piri Thomas.	Enables students to understand the complex ways in which diverse racial and cultural groups participated in the formation of U.S. society and culture. Helps reduce racial and ethnic encapsulation. Enables diverse ethnic, racial, and religious groups to see their cultures, ethos, and perspectives in the school curriculum. Gives students a balanced view of the nature and development of U.S. culture and society. Helps to empower victimized racial, ethnic, and cultural groups.	The implementation of this approach requires substantial curriculum revision, in-service training, and the identification and development of materials written from the perspectives of various racial and cultural groups. Staff development for the institutionalization of this approach must be continual and ongoing.
Social Action	In this approach, students identify important social problems and issues, gather pertinent data, clarify their values on the issues, make decisions, and take reflective actions to help resolve the issue or problem.	A class studies prejudice and discrimination in its school and decides to take actions to improve race relations in the school. A class studies the treatment of ethnic groups in a local newspaper and writes a letter to the publisher suggesting ways that the treatment of ethnic groups in the newspaper should be improved.	Enables students to improve their thinking, value analysis, decision-making and social-action skills. Enables students to improve their data-gathering skills. Helps students develop a sense of political efficacy. Helps students improve their skills to work in groups.	Requires a considerable amount of curriculum planning and materials identification. May be longer in duration than more traditional teaching units. May focus on problems and issues considered controversial by some members of the school staff and citizens of the community. Students may be able to take few meaningful actions that contribute to the resolution of the social issue or problem.

Appendix C

Creating a Multicultural Context for the Cases

All of the cases will generate a richer and more meaningful discussion if set in an authentic educational and cultural context. To that end, several options are possible:

Scenario 1: Decide that the school and classroom in which the case takes place are quite diverse—with proportions of students of color, lower socioeconomic status, disability, and the like *greater than those of the general population.* (See Tables 1.1 and 1.2 for estimated populations of minority groups in the United States.)

Scenario 2: Specify that the diversity in the community, school, and classroom in which the case takes place is *equal to that of the general population.*

Scenario 3: Specify that the diversity in the case school is equal to that of the school in which you are completing or have completed a field experience. It is recommended that this option be selected only when a specific and significant need suggests it. For example, if a school in which you work as a teacher's aide, a student teacher, or a teacher is 98 percent white and has recently experienced racial tension, you might decide to analyze a given case with racial issues within this setting.

In addition to the types of diversity outlined in the tables, students in schools vary in other ways, including language, religious affiliation, and gender. The reader is referred to multicultural education sources for statistics on other groups and for additional data on the groups cited earlier.

Based on the percentages of various groups in the United States as listed in Tables 1.1 and 1.2, the composition of a "typical" classroom of 30* students would be as shown in Table 1.3:

Obviously, such a "typical" class will rarely exist. It is constructed here for those who would want to set the cases provided in a classroom that represents the diversity of persons in the general population.

*A given student may well belong to more than one group; therefore, the total number of students listed exceeds 30.

Table 1.1 Estimated Population of Ethnic Groups in the United States, According to Race, Hispanic Origin, and Jewish and Muslim Origin, 1990

Race	Percentage
All Persons	**100.0**
White Americans	80.3
African Americans	12.1
American Indian, Eskimo, or Aleut	0.8
American Indians	0.8
Aleuts	0.0
Asian or Pacific Islander	2.9
Chinese Americans	0.7
Japanese Americans	0.3
Asian Indian	0.3
Korean Americans	0.3
Vietnamese	0.2
Native Hawaiians	0.1
Samoans	0.0
Guamanians	0.0
Other Asian or Pacific Islander	0.3
Other	3.9
Hispanic Origin	
All Persons	**100.0**
Hispanic Origin	9.0
Mexican	5.4
Puerto Rican	1.1
Cuban	0.4
Other Hispanic	2.0
Not of Hispanic Origin	91.0
Jewish and Muslim Origin	
All Persons	**100.0**
Jewish	2.8
Muslim	2.1

Source: Bennett, C. L. *Comprehensive Multicultural Education: Theory and Practice* (3rd ed.). Copyright ©1995 by Allyn and Bacon. Reprinted/adapted by permission.

Table 1.2 Estimated Percentage of Children in Poverty, with Disabilities, and of Gay/Lesbian/Bisexual Orientation

Poverty	Percentage
Children under age of 18 who are poor (Reed & Sautter, 1990)	20
Exceptionality	
Children identified as disabled for purposes of special education services (U.S. Department of Education, 1994)	12
Affectional Orientation	
Persons of gay/lesbian/bisexual orientation (Kalota et al., 1994)	10

Table 1.3 Composition of a Classroom of 30 Students*

Students	Number
White	24
African American	4
Asian	1
American Indian	1
Hispanic	3
Jewish	1
Muslim	1
Poor	6
Disabled	2–3
Gay/lesbian/bisexual	3

*Based on estimated population of ethnic, socioeconomic class, poverty, exceptionability, and affectional orientation

Because the student bodies in many schools consist of much greater proportions of ethnic diversity than that of the general population, when analyzing a given case, you should assume that the story takes place in such a school. Doing so will better prepare you for a career that might well include teaching in a school with a rich diversity of students.

Once you have predetermined the ethnic, socioeconomic, religious, exceptionality, and affectional orientation of the students in a case, establish other classroom, school, and community characteristics that will further provide the context for the case. For example, specify factors such as the

- Number of students served in the school
- Number of students in the particular classroom
- School budget
- Performance levels of students on statewide achievement tests

Furthermore, determine if the school

- Tracks students into several levels
- Has access to tutors and student teachers in a teacher education program in a local college
- Has class periods of a certain length, for example, 50, 60, or 90 minutes
- Has stand-alone and on-line access to sophisticated computer and related technologies
- Has a well-developed parent-involvement program

Examples of contexts that might be designed as a basis for the analysis of a given case follow.

Example I

Longfellow Elementary School serves 1,000 low and low-middle socioeconomic status students living in the inner city. Typical classroom size is 25 students per room. The student body is 40 percent African American, 10 percent Hispanic, 5 percent Asian, 5 percent Native American, and 40 percent white. Approximately 20 percent of the students are Jewish. Student scores on standardized achievement tests are in the 90th percentile. The school divides students into three tracks. Thirty-nine percent of graduates go on to college. Reform efforts have moved the school to the fore in terms of offering a well-developed multicultural curriculum.

Example II

Lincoln Elementary School serves 500 low-SES pupils. The student body is 70 percent white, 20 percent Native American, and 10 percent African American. Approximately 40 percent of the students come from farms around the city of 40,000. Fifty percent of pupils come from single-parent families, and half are from families that claim to be devoutly Catholic. Class size in Lincoln is 30 students per room. Each room has two computers with Internet interface, and two computer labs of 20 computers each are available to teachers. Except for the progressive approach to technology, the curriculum is relatively traditional. Parent involvement in school activities is low.

Each of these examples emphasizes different characteristics in terms of ethnicity, SES, religion, family structure, curriculum, and the like. Each could have been more or less elaborate, depending on the nature of the case to be analyzed, the needs and interests of the students analyzing the case, and the goals of the course or workshop within which the case is used.

Teachers who have used case studies have reported added benefits from discussing the same case within several different cultural and educational contexts thereby illustrating the importance of context on case analysis.

References

Kolata, G., Laumann, E., Michael, R., & Gagnon, J. (1994). *Sex in America.* Chicago: National Opinion Research Center, University of Chicago.

Reed, S., & Sautter, R. (1990). Children of poverty—The status of 12 million young Americans. *Phi Delta Kappan, 71*(10), K1–K12.

U.S. Department of Education. (1994). *Sixteenth annual report to congress on the implementation of the Individuals with Disabilities Education Act.* Washington, DC: U.S. Government Printing Office. Cited in Banks, J.A., & Banks, C.A. McGee (1997). *Multicultural education: Issues and perspectives.* Boston: Allyn & Bacon, p. 308.

Bibliography

Anderson, E. M., Redman, G. L., & Rogers, C. (1991). *Self-esteem for tots to teens.* Wayzata, MN: Parenting and Teaching Publications.

Banks, J. A. (1994). *An introduction to multicultural education.* Boston: Allyn & Bacon.

Banks, J.A. (1994). *Multiethnic education.* Boston: Allyn & Bacon.

Banks, J.A. & Banks, C. A. M. (Eds.). (1997). *Multicultural education: Issues and perspectives,* Boston: Allyn & Bacon.

Battle, J. (1987). Relationship between self-esteem and depression among children. *Psycholgical Reports, 60* (3, part 2), 1187–1190.

Beane, J., & Lipka, R. (1984). *Self-concept, self-esteem, and the curriculum.* Newton, MA: Allyn & Bacon.

Bennett, C. (1995). *Comprehensive multicultural education theory and practice.* Needham Heights, MA: Allyn & Bacon.

Chisholm, I. M. (1994). Culture and technology: Implications for multicultural teacher education. *Journal of Information Technology and Teacher Education* 3 (2), 213–228.

Christensen, L. (1994). Unlearning the myths that bind us. In Rethinking our classrooms: Teaching for equity and justice (pp. 8–13). Milwaukee, WI: Rethinking Our Schools Ltd.

Clark, C., & Lampert, M. (1986). The study of teacher thinking: Implications for teacher education. *Journal of Teacher Education,* 37(5), 27–31.

Cooper, J. M. (1995). Teacher's problem solving: A casebook of award-winning cases. Needham Heights, MA: Allyn & Bacon.

Covington, M. (1984). *The self-worth theory of motivation, The Elementary School Journal,* 85 (1), 5–20.

Danielson, C. (1996). *Enhancing professional practice: A framework for teaching.* Alexandria, VA: Association for Supervision and Curriculum Development.

Davis, L. (1996, April). Equality in education: An agenda for urban schools. *Equity & Excellence in Education,* pp. 61–67.

Feagin, J. & Feagin, C. (1993). *Racial and ethnic relations* (4th ed.). Englewood Cliffs, NJ: Prentice Hall.

Frey, D., & Carlock, C.J. (1989). *Enhancing self-esteem.* Muncie, IN: Accelerated Development Publishers.

Gage, N. L. (1978). *The scientific basis of the art of teaching.* New York: Teachers College Press.

Glasser, W. (1985). *Control theory in the classroom.* New York: Perennial Library.

Greenwood, G. E., & Fillmer, H. T. (1997). *Professional core cases for teacher decision-making.* Upper Saddle River, NJ: Prentice Hall.

Hunt, D. E., & Sullivan, E. V. (1974). *Between psychology and education.* New York: Holt, Rinehart and Winston.

Kennedy, M. M. (1991). *An agenda for research on teacher learning.* (Special Report). East Lansing, MI: National Center for Research on Teacher Learning.

Kleinfeld, J. (1992). Learning to think like a teacher: The study of cases. In J. H. Shulman (Ed.), *Case methods in teacher education* (pp. 33-49). New York: Teachers College Press.

Kolata, G., Laumann, E., Michael, R., & Gagnon, J. (1994). *Sex in America*. Chicago: National Opinion Research Center, University of Chicago.

Kosmin, Barry A. et al. (1991). *Highlights of the CJF 1990 national Jewish population survey.* New York: Council of Jewish Federation, pp. 3-6, 10, 20-22, 25-26. Reprinted in J. Feagin & C. Feagin (1993), *Racial and ethnic relations* (4th ed.,p. 172). Englewood Cliffs, NJ: Prentice Hall.

Lay, R., & Wakstein, J. R. (1985). Academic achievement, and self-concept of ability. *Research in High Education, 22,* 43-64.

McNergney, R., Herbert, J., & Ford, R. (1994). Cooperation and competition in cases-based education. *Journal of Teacher Education, 45*(5), 339-345.

Marzano, R. J. (1992). *A different kind of classroom: Teaching with dimensions of learning.* Arlington, VA: Association for Supervision and Curriculum Development.

Merseth, K. K. (1991). *The case for cases in teacher education.* Washington, DC: American Association for Higher Education and the American Association of Colleges for Teacher Education.

Morine-Dershimer, G. (1985). *Talking, listening, and learning.* New York: Longman.

Morine-Dershimer, G. (1991). Learning to think like a teacher. *Teaching and Teacher Education, 7*(2), 159-168.

Oja, S., & Sprinthall, N. A. (1978). Psychological and moral development for teachers. In N. A. Sprinthall & R. L. Mosher (Eds.), *Value development as the aim of education* (pp. 117-134). Schenectady, NY: Charter Research Press.

Peterson, P. L., Carpenter, T., & Fennema, E. (1989). Teachers' knowledge of students' knowledge in mathematics problem solving: Correlational and case analysis. *Journal of Educational Psychology, 81,* 558-569.

Pusch, M. D. (Ed.). (1979). *Multicultural education: A cross cultural training approach.* Yarmouth, ME: Intercultural Press.

Redman, G. L. (1995). *Building self-esteem in children: A skill and strategy workbook for parents.* Wayzata, MN: Parenting and Teaching Publications .

Redman, G. L. (1992). *Building self-esteem in students: A skill and strategy workbook for teachers.* Wayzata, MN: Parenting and Teaching Publications.

Reed, S., & Sautter, R. (1990). Children of poverty—the status of 12 million young Americans. *Phi Delta Kappa, 71*(10), K1-K12.

Riley, S. S. (1984). *How to generate values in young children: Integrity, honesty, individuality, self-confidence, and wisdom.* Washington, DC: National Association for the Education of Young Children.

Rosenberg, M., & Pearlin, L. I. (1982). Social class and self-esteem among children and adults. In M. Rosenberg & H. B. Kaplan (Eds.), *Social psychology of the self-concept* (pp. 268-288). Arlington Heights, IL: Harlan Davidson.

Shulman, L., (1992). Toward a pedagogy of cases. In J. H. Shulman (Ed.), *Case methods in teacher education.* New York: Teachers College Press.

Schon, D. A. (1987) *Educating the reflective practitioner.* San Francisco: Jossey-Bass.

Silverman, R., Welty, W., & Lyon, S. (1994). *Multicultural education cases for teacher problem solving.* New York: McGraw-Hill.

Silverman, R., Welty, W. & Lyon, S. (1994). *Teaching methods cases for teacher problem solving.* New York: McGraw-Hill.

Sprinthall, N.A. & Thies-Sprinthall, L. (1983). The teacher as an adult learner: A cognitive-developmental view. *National Society for the Study of Education Yearbook,* Pt. 2, 13-35.

Tenth Annual Report to Congress on the Implementation of the Handicapped Act. (1988). Washington, DC: U.S. Department of Education.

The Truth About Teachers. Pyramid Film and Video, Santa Monica, CA.

Trudgill, P. (1984). *Sociolinguistics: An introduction to language and society.* New York: Penguin Books.

Understanding Islam and the Muslims (1989). Washington, DC: The Embassy of Saudi Arabia. Reprinted in Bennett, C. (1995). *Comprehensive multicultural education theory and practice.* Needham Heights, MA: Allyn & Bacon.

Reviews

Anderson, L. M., Blumenfeld, P., Pintrich, P. R., Clark, C. M., Marx, R. W., & Peterson, P. (1995). Educational psychology for teachers: Reforming our courses, rethinking our roles. *Educational Psychologist, 30*(3), 143-158.

Harrington, H., & Garrison, M. (1992). Cases as shared inquiry: A dialogical model of teacher preparation. *American Educational Research Journal, 29,* 715-735.

Merseth, K. (1996). Cases and case methods in teacher education. In J. Sikula (Ed.), *Handbook of research on teacher education* (pp. 722-746). New York: Macmillan/Simon & Shuster.

Empirical Studies

Levin, B. B. (1994). Using the case method in teacher education: The role of discussion and experience in teachers' thinking about cases. *Teacher and Teacher Education, 10*(2), 1-17.

Levin, B. B. (1996, April). *Learning from discussion: A comparison of computer-based versus face-to-face case discussions.* Paper presented at American Educational Research Association Conference, New York.

Lundeberg, M. A. (1993). Case discussions in educational psychology. In V. Wolf (Ed.), *Improving the climate of the college classroom* (pp. 159-164). Madison: University of Wisconsin System Office of Equal Opportunity Programs and Policy Studies.

Lundeberg, M.A., & Fawver, J. E. (1994). Thinking like a teacher: Encouraging cognitive growth in case analysis. *Journal of Teacher Education, 45*(4), 289-297.

Lundeberg, M.A., Matthews, D., & Scheurman, G. (1996,). *Looking twice means seeing more: How knowledge affects case analysis.* Paper presented at the American Educational Research Association Conference, New York.

Books on Reflective Thinking and Case Methods

Christensen, C. R., & Hansen, A. J. (1986). *Teaching and the case method.* Boston: Harvard Business School Publishing Division.

Christensen, C. R., Hansen, A. J., & Moore, J. F. (1986). *Teaching and the case method instructor's guide.* Boston: Harvard Business School Publishing Division.

Erskine, J. A., Leenders, M. R., & Mauffette-Leenders, L. A. (1981). *Teaching with cases.* London, Ontario, Canada: Research and Publication Division, School of Business Administration, The University of Western Ontario.

Greenwood, G., & Parkay, F. W. (1989). *Case studies for teacher decision making.* New York: Random House.

Grossman, P. L. (1990). *The making of a teacher: Teacher knowledge and teacher education.* New York: Teachers College Press.

Huntchings, P. (1993). *Using cases to improve college teaching: A guide to more reflective practice.* Washington, DC: American Association for Higher Education.

Kagan, D. M., & Tippins, D. J. (1993). Classroom cases as gauges of professional growth. In M. O'Hair & S. Odell (Eds.), *Teacher education yearbook 1: Diversity and teaching* (pp. 98-110). New York: Harcourt Brace Jovanovich and the Association of Teacher Educators.

Merseth, K. (1991). *The case for cases in teacher education.* Washington, DC: American Association for Higher Education.

Schon, D. A. (1983). *The reflective practitioner: How professions think in action.* New York: Basic Books.

Schon, D. A. (1991). *The reflective turn: Case studies in and on educational practice.* New York: Teachers College Press.

Schulman, J. H. (Ed.). (1992). *Case methods in teacher education.* New York: Teachers College Press.

Schulman, J. H., & Mesa-Bains, A. (Eds.). (1993). *Diversity in the classroom: A casebook for teachers and teacher educators.* Hillsdale, NJ: Research for Better Schools and Lawrence Erlbaum Associates.

Silverman, R., Welty, W., & Lyon, S. (1996). *Case studies for teacher problem solving* (2nd ed.). New York: McGraw-Hill.

Silverman, R., Welty, W., & Lyon, S. (1994). *Classroom assessment cases for teacher problem solving.* New York: McGraw-Hill.

Silverman, R., Welty, W., & Lyon, S. (1994). *Classroom management cases for teacher problem solving.* New York: McGraw-Hill.

Silverman, R., Welty, W., & Lyon, S. (1994). *Educational psychology cases for teacher problem solving.* New York: McGraw-Hill.

Silverman, R., Welty, W., & Lyon, S. (1994). *Multicultural education cases for teacher problem solving.* New York: McGraw-Hill.

Silverman, R., Welty, W., & Lyon, S. (1994). *Primis education series: Case studies for teacher problem solving.* New York: McGraw-Hill.

Wasserman, S. (1993). *Getting down to cases.* New York: Teachers College Press.

Journal Articles and Papers

Albanese, M., & Mitchell, S. (1993). Problem-based learning: A review of literature on its outcomes and implementation issues. *Academic Medicine, 68*, 52-81.

Fourtner, A. W., Fourtner, C. R., & Herreid, C. F. (1994). Bad blood: A study of the Tuskegee syphilis project. *Journal of College Science Teaching, 23*, 277-285.

Harrington, H. L. (1994). Perspectives on cases. *International Journal of Qualitative Studies in Education, 7*(2), 117-133.

Harrington, H. L., & Garrison, J. (1992). Cases as shared inquiry: A dialogical model of teacher preparation. *American Educational Research Journal, 29*(4), 715-735.

Herreid, C. F. (1994). Case studies in science: A novel method of science education. *Journal of College Science Teaching, 23*, 221-229.

Kagan, D. M., & Tippins, D. J. (1991). How teachers' classrooms cases express their pedagogical beliefs. *Journal of Teacher Education, 42*(4), 281-291.

Kagan, D. M. (1993). Contexts for the use of classroom cases. *American Educational Research Journal, 30*(4), 703-723.

Kleinfeld, J. (1990). *Creating cases on your own.* Fairbanks: Department of Education, Rural College, University of Alaska.

Kleinfeld, J. (1990). The special virtues of the case method in preparing teachers for minority schools. *Teacher Education Quarterly, 17*(1), 43-51.

Mason, C. (1981). *Notes to a beginning case method teacher.* Boston: Harvard Business School Publishing Division. Case #381-007.

Merseth, K. K., & Lacey, C. A. (1993). Weaving stronger fabric: The pedagogical promise of hypermedia and case methods in teacher education. *Teaching & Teacher Education, 9*(3), 283-299.

Shapiro, B. (1984). *An introduction to cases.* Boston: Harvard Business School Publishing Division. Case #584-097.

Sykes, G., & Bird, T. (1992). Teacher education and the case idea. *Review of Research in Education, 18*, 457-521.

Sources of Cases

Case Program Sales Office
Kennedy School of Government
Harvard University
79 John F. Kennedy Street
Cambridge, MA 02138
617-495-9523
fax: 617-495-8878
ksg.harvard.edu/caseweb/

Center for Case Studies in Education
Pace University
861 Bedford Road
Pleasantville, NY 10570-2799
914-773-3879
fax: 914-773-3878
silverma@pace.edu

EDI Case Collection
World Bank
http://www.worldbank.org/html/edi/cases/caseindex/html

Harvard Business School Publishing
Customer Service Department
Boston, MA 02163
800-545-7685
fax: 617-495-6985
http://www.hbsp.harvard.edu

Institute for the Study of Diplomacy
Pew Case Study Center
School of Foreign Service
Georgetown University
Washington, DC 20057-1052
202-965-5735 ext. 3005 (Pete Paraschos)
fax: 202-687-8312
http://sfswww.georgetown.edu/sfs/programs/isd/pub.html

The Johns Hopkins Foreign Policy Institute
FPI Publications Program
School of Advanced International Studies
1740 Massachusetts Ave. N.W.
Washington, DC 20036

Program for Decision Cases
(agricultural and natural resource cases)
University of Minnesota
College of Agriculture
411 Borlaug Hall
St. Paul, MN 55108-6026
612-624-1211

Books Containing Case Studies

Emmer, E. T., Evertson, C. M., Sanford, J. P., Clements, B. S., & Worsham, M. E.
   (1989). *Classroom management for secondary teachers*. Englewood
   Cliffs, NJ: Prentice Hall.
Green, G. E., & Parkay, F. W. (1989). *Case studies for teacher decision
   making*. New York: Random House.

Greenwood, G. E., & Fillmer, H. T. (1997). *Professional Core Cases for Teacher Decision-Making.* Upper Saddle River, NJ: Prentice Hall.

Hinely, R., & Ford, K. (1995). *Education in Edge City: Cases for reflection and action.* New York: St. Martin's Press.

Kaufman, J. M., Mostert, M. P., Nuttycombe, D. G., Trent, S. C., & Hallahan, D. P. (1993). *Managing classroom behavior: A reflective case-based approach.* Boston: Allyn & Bacon.

Kleinfeld, J. (Ed.). (1988). *Teaching cases in cross-cultural education.* Fairbanks, AL: College of Education.

Kowalski, T. J., Weaver, R. A., & Henson, K. T. (1990). *Case studies on teaching.* New York: Longman.

Merseth, K. K. (Ed.). (in press). *Cases for decisions in teacher education.* New York: HarperCollins.

Nieto, S. *Affirming diversity.* New York: Longman.

Wasserman, S. (1993). *Getting down to cases: Learning to teach with case studies.* New York: Teachers College Press.

Watson, C. R. (1997). *Middle school case studies.* Upper Saddle River, NJ: Prentice-Hall.

Internet Resources

General Educational Resources

Children Now	http://www.dnai.com/~children/
Edweb	http://edweb.gsn.org/
ERIC	http://ericir.syr.edu
	(lesson plans, database, etc.)
Internet Public Library	http://www.ipl.org/ref/
U.S. Dept. of Education	http://www.ed.gov/
WWW Virtual Library	vlib.stanford.edu/overview.html

Teaching with Technology

T.H.E. Online	http://www.thejournal.com
	(*Journal of Technology in Higher Education*)
Teaching with Technology	http:/www.uvm.edu/~jmorris/
Web 66	http://web66.coled.umn.edu
	(to set up web servers)

Lesson Plan and Curriculum Sites

ERIC	http://ericir.syr.edu/Virtual
	(choose lesson plans)
Busy Teacher's page	http://www.ceismc.gatech.edu/BusyT
Classroom Connect	http://www.classroom.net/
Curriculum Connections	http://www.ala.org/ICONN/curricuz.html
Curriculum Guides, etc.	http://libinfo.ume.maine.edu/LMC/currguid.htm
Curriculum Web Page	http://www.luc.edu/libraries/maillinckrodt/index/html

Discovery Channel School   http://www.school.discovery.
                                  com/
Pitsco's Launch to Ed...   http://http://pitsco.inter.net/
                                  pitsco/p/resource.html
Teacher's Forum   http://education.indiana.edu/
                                  cas/ttforum.html
Teacher's helping teachers   http://www.pacificnet.net/
                                  ~mandel
World Lecture Hall   http://www.civeng.carleton.ca/
                                  ~nholtz/tut/doc/doc.html
Writing Opportunities   http://192.41.39.106/young/
Inkspot for young writers

Children's Literature Web Sites

Children's Lit Web   http://www.acs.ucalgary.ca/
                                ~dkbrown
                                http://www.carolhurst.com/

Journals

Electronic Journals   http://aera.net/pubs/aerj/
                                index.html

Newspapers

Hot links to U.S. and   http:www.naa.org/hot
foreign newspapers

Reference Sources

Review of Websites   http://www.pointcom.com
                                (Top 5% of sites)
The Weather Channel   http://weather.com

Searching the Web

Internet Tool Box   http://www.library.umass.edu

Education and Cultural Diversity

Teacher Training and   http://unesco.uneb.edu/
Multiculturalism   educnews/multiculturalism/
                                http://wwwvaldosta.peachnet.
                                edu/~whuitt/edu.html#mc

Internet Projects

Global SchoolNet's   http://www.gsn.org/gsn/proj/
Internet Project   index.html
Registry
KIDPROS   http://www.kidlink.org:80/
                                KIDPROJ/